Apr. 12, 2010

D1455367

GOD
NEVER
BLINKS

GOD
NEVER
BLINKS

*50 Lessons for Life's
Little Detours*

REGINA BRETT

GRAND CENTRAL
PUBLISHING

New York Boston

Grand Central Publishing
Hachette Book Group
237 Park Avenue
New York, NY 10017
www.HachetteBookGroup.com

Printed in the United States of America

First Edition: April 2010

10 9 8 7 6 5 4 3 2 1

Grateful acknowledgment is made to quote from the following:

Columns that originally appeared in the *Plain Dealer* are reprinted with permission of the Plain Dealer Publishing Co. The *Plain Dealer* holds the copright for columns written by Regina Brett from 2000 to 2009. All rights reserved.

Columns that originally appeared in the *Beacon Journal* are reprinted with permission from the Beacon Journal Publishing Co. Inc. The *Beacon Journal* holds the copyright for columns written by Regina Brett from 1994 to 2000. All rights reserved.

Lines from "A Father's Story" by Andre Dubus, *The Times Are Never So Bad*, copyright © 1983 (Boston: David R. Godine, Publisher, Inc., 1983) are reprinted by permission.

The excerpt from *Alcoholics Anonymous* is reprinted with permission of Alcoholics Anonymous World Services, Inc. ("AAWS"). Permission to reprint this excerpt, which orginally ran on page 552 of the Third Edition, does not mean that AAWS has reviewed or approved the contents of this publication, or that AAWS necessarily agrees with the views expressed herein. A.A. is a program of recovery from alcoholism *only* – use of this excerpt in connection with programs and activities that are patterned after A.A., but that address other problems, or in any other non-A.A context, does not imply otherwise.

David Chilton, *The Wealthy Barber: The Common Sense Guide to Successful Financial Planning* (New York: Three Rivers Press, 1998). Excerpt used by permission.

Pastor Rick Warren for permission to use the quote in Lesson 31.

Grand Central Publishing is a division of Hachette Book Group, Inc.
The Grand Central Publishing name and logo is a trademark of Hachette Book Group, Inc.

Library of Congress Cataloging-in-Publication Data

Brett, Regina.
    God never blinks : 50 lessons for life's little detours / Regina Brett. — 1st ed.
        p. cm.
    ISBN 978-0-446-55652-1
    1. Life skills.   2. Quality of life.   3. Conduct of life.   I. Title.
HQ2037.B745 2010
646.7 — dc22

2009027123

Book design by Giorgetta Bell McRee

For Asher
and Julia

my bookends

Contents

Introduction   *1*

The Fifty Lessons   *5*

Lesson 1   Life isn't fair, but it's still good.   *7*

Lesson 2   When in doubt, just take the next right step.   *10*

Lesson 3   Life is too short to waste time hating anyone.   *15*

Lesson 4   Don't take yourself so seriously. No one else does.   *19*

Lesson 5   Pay off your credit cards every month.   *24*

Contents

Lesson 6   You don't have to win every argument. Agree to disagree. *28*

Lesson 7   Cry with someone. It's more healing than crying alone. *33*

Lesson 8   It's okay to get angry with God. He can take it. *37*

Lesson 9   The most important sex organ is the brain. *42*

Lesson 10   God never gives us more than we were designed to carry. *47*

Lesson 11   Make peace with your past so it doesn't screw up the present. *51*

Lesson 12   It's okay to let your children see you cry. *56*

Lesson 13   Don't compare your life to others'. You have no idea what their journey is all about. *60*

Lesson 14   If a relationship has to be kept secret, you shouldn't be in it. *65*

Lesson 15   Everything can change in the blink of an eye. But don't worry; God never blinks. *70*

Lesson 16   Life is too short for long pity parties. Get busy living, or get busy dying. *74*

Lesson 17   You can get through anything life hands you if you stay put in the day you are in and don't jump ahead. *78*

Contents

Lesson 18 A writer is someone who writes. If you want to be a writer, write. *82*

Lesson 19 It's never too late to have a happy childhood. But the second one is up to you and no one else. *87*

Lesson 20 When it comes to going after what you love in life, don't take no for an answer. *92*

Lesson 21 Burn the candles, use the nice sheets, wear the fancy lingerie. Don't save anything for a special occasion. Today is special enough. *97*

Lesson 22 Overprepare, then go with the flow. *102*

Lesson 23 Be eccentric now. Don't wait for old age to wear purple. *106*

Lesson 24 Start saving 10 percent for retirement as soon as you get your first paycheck. *111*

Lesson 25 No one else is in charge of your happiness. You are the CEO of your joy. *115*

Lesson 26 Frame every so-called disaster with these words: "In five years, will this matter?" *119*

Lesson 27 Always choose life. *124*

Lesson 28 Forgive everyone everything. *128*

Lesson 29 What other people think of you is none of your business. *133*

Contents

Lesson 30 The passage of time heals almost everything. Give time time. *138*

Lesson 31 No matter how good or how bad a situation is, it will change. *143*

Lesson 32 Your job won't take care of you when you are sick, but your friends will. Stay in touch with them. *148*

Lesson 33 Believe in miracles. *152*

Lesson 34 God loves you because of who God is, not because of anything you did or didn't do. *155*

Lesson 35 Whatever doesn't kill you really does make you stronger. *160*

Lesson 36 Growing old beats the alternative. Dying young looks good only in movies. *165*

Lesson 37 Your children get only one childhood. Make it memorable. *170*

Lesson 38 Read the Psalms. No matter what your faith, they cover every human emotion. *175*

Lesson 39 Get outside every day. Miracles are waiting for you to discover. *179*

Lesson 40 If we all threw our problems in a pile and got a look at everyone else's, we'd fight to get back our own. *183*

Contents

Lesson 41 Don't audit life. Show up and make the most of now. *188*

Lesson 42 Get rid of anything that isn't useful, beautiful, or joyful. *191*

Lesson 43 All that truly matters in the end is that you loved. *194*

Lesson 44 Envy is a waste of time. You already have everything you truly need. *198*

Lesson 45 The best is yet to come. *202*

Lesson 46 No matter how you feel, get up, dress up, and show up for life. *210*

Lesson 47 Breathe. It calms the mind. *214*

Lesson 48 If you don't ask, you don't get. *218*

Lesson 49 Yield. *223*

Lesson 50 Life isn't tied with a bow, but it's still a gift. *229*

Author's Note *235*

Acknowledgments *237*

About the Author *241*

GOD
NEVER
BLINKS

Introduction

My friend Kathy once sent me an excerpt from the book *Dandelion Wine*. In Ray Bradbury's book about one vintage summer, a boy has taken ill. No one can figure out what is wrong. He's simply overwhelmed by life. No one seems able to help him until Mr. Jonas, the junk man, comes along.

He whispers to the boy who lies asleep on a cot in the yard. Mr. Jonas tells him to rest quiet and listen, then reaches up and picks an apple off a tree. He lingers long enough to tell the boy a secret he carries inside him, one I didn't know I carried in me. Some folks arrive in this world fragile. Like tender fruit, they bruise easier, cry more often, and turn sad young. Mr. Jonas knows all this because he's one of those people.

The words stir something in the boy and he recovers.

The words stirred something in me. Some people bruise easier. I'm one of those people.

Introduction

It took me 40 years to find and hold on to happiness. I always felt that at the moment I was born, God must have blinked. He missed the occasion and never knew I had arrived. My parents had 11 children. While I love my parents and my five brothers and five sisters deeply, some days I felt lost in the litter. As Kathy often pointed out, I seemed to be the runt of that litter. I ended up confused by the nuns at age 6, a lost soul who drank too much at 16, an unwed mother at 21, a college graduate at 30, a single mother for 18 years, and finally, a wife at 40, married to a man who treated me like a queen.

Then I got cancer at 41. It took a year to fight it, then a year to recover from the fight.

When I turned 45, I lay in bed reflecting on all life had taught me. My soul sprang a leak and ideas flowed out. My pen simply caught them and set the words on paper. I typed them up and turned them into a newspaper column of the 45 lessons life taught me. My editor hated it. So did his editor. I asked them to run it anyway. The *Plain Dealer* readers in Cleveland loved it.

Cancer made me bold enough to speak up to the bosses. Once you've had cancer and been sick, bald, and weak from chemotherapy and radiation, there aren't a lot worse things anyone can do to you. Turning 45 was a victory for me. Breast cancer left me doubting I would see the odometer roll over that far. Three of my aunts died from it at 42, 44, and 56, so it didn't look good.

But I kept living. When I hit 50, I added five more lessons and the paper ran the column again. Then something amazing happened. People across the country began to forward the column. Ministers, nurses, and social workers requested reprints to run in newsletters, church bulletins, and small-town newspapers. People of all religions and those of none at all could relate. While some of the lessons speak of God, people found in them universal truths. I've heard from agnostics and atheists who carry the list of lessons in their wallets and keep it tacked to their work cubicles and stuck under refrigerator magnets. The lessons are posted on blogs and websites by people all over the world. Every week since the column ran, people have e-mailed from Australia to Zanesville, Ohio, asking for copies. That column is the most popular one I've written in my 24 years as a journalist.

Most of these essays originally appeared in the *Plain Dealer* or the *Beacon Journal*. Some of them are originals.

These lessons are life's gifts to me, and mine to you.

The
Fifty
Lessons

Life Isn't Fair, but It's Still Good.

The hat always came back, more faded yet stronger than ever.

Frank started it.

I had undergone my first chemotherapy and couldn't imagine being bald. Then I saw a guy wearing a baseball cap bearing these words: LIFE IS GOOD.

Life didn't feel good and it was about to feel worse, so I asked the guy where he got the hat. Two days later, Frank drove across town and stopped by my house and gave me one. Frank is a magical kind of guy. A house painter by trade, he lives by two simple words: *Get to.*

They remind him to be grateful for everything. Instead of saying, "I have to go to work today," Frank tells himself, "I get to go to work." Instead of saying, "I have to get groceries," he gets to. Instead of saying, "I have to take the kids to baseball practice," he gets to. It works for everything.

The hat on anyone but Frank might not have carried the same power. It was navy blue with an oval patch that announced its message in white letters.

And life was good. Even though my hair fell out, my body grew weak, my eyebrows fell off. Instead of wearing a wig, I wore that hat as my answer to cancer, as my billboard to the world. People love to stare at a bald woman. They got a message back when they gawked.

Gradually, I got well, my hair grew back, and I put the hat away until a friend got cancer and asked about that hat I used to wear. She wanted one. At first I didn't want to part with mine. It was like my binky, my security blanket. But I had to pass it on. If I didn't, the luck might run out. She made a promise to get well and pass the hat on to another woman. Instead, she gave it back to me to pass on to another survivor.

We call it the Chemo Hat.

I don't know how many women have worn it these past 11 years. I've lost count. So many friends have been diagnosed with breast cancer. Arlene. Joy. Cheryl. Kaye. Sheila. Joan. Sandy. Woman after woman passed it on.

When the hat came back to me, it always looked more tired and worn, but each woman had a new sparkle in her eyes. Everyone who wore the lucky Chemo Hat is still alive and thriving.

Last year I gave it to my friend and coworker Patrick. He was diagnosed with colon cancer at age 37. Patrick got the hat, even though I wasn't sure it could tackle any kind of cancer. He told his mom about the hat, how he was now a link in this chain of survival. She found Life is good, Inc., the company that made the hat and makes other products with the motto. She called the company and told them the story of the hat and ordered a whole box of caps.

She sent them to Patrick's closest friends and relatives. They took pictures of themselves wearing the hats. All over his refrigerator he put up photos of college friends and their kids and dogs and lawn ornaments wearing the LIFE IS GOOD hat.

Meanwhile, the folks at Life is good, Inc., were moved by Patrick's mom. They held a staff meeting and challenged their employees, "in the spirit of the traveling lucky Chemo Hat," to pass their hats on to someone needing a lift. They sent Patrick a photo of all 175 of them each wearing a hat.

Patrick finished chemo and is fine. He was so lucky; he never lost his hair, it just thinned out. He never wore the hat, but it touched him. He kept it on a table at the bottom of the stairs where he could see that message every day.

It got him through the really bad days when he wanted to quit chemo and give up. Anyone with cancer has known those days. Even folks who have never had cancer have known them.

Turns out it wasn't the hat but the message on it that kept us all going, that keeps us all going.

Life *is* good.

Pass it on.

When in Doubt, Just Take the Next Right Step.

My life used to be like that game of freeze tag we played as kids. Once tagged, you had to freeze in the position you were in. Whenever something happened, I'd freeze like a statue, too afraid of moving the wrong way, too afraid of making the wrong decision. The problem is, if you stand still too long, *that's* your decision.

There's a moment in the special *A Charlie Brown Christmas* where Charlie Brown stops to see Lucy, the five-cent psychiatrist. Lucy does her best to diagnosis him.

If he's afraid of responsibility, he must have hypengyophobia. Charlie Brown isn't sure if that's exactly what he fears the most.

Lucy tries hard to put her finger on it. If he's afraid of staircases, he could have climacophobia. If he's afraid of the ocean, he has thalassophobia. Maybe it's gephyrophobia, the fear of crossing bridges.

Finally, Lucy hits on just the right diagnosis: panophobia.

When she asks Charlie Brown if that's what he has, he asks her what it is. The answer both shocks and comforts him.

What is panophobia? The fear of *everything*.

Bingo! That's what Charlie Brown has.

Me, too.

I stumbled through high school using alcohol as my compass. I went to college in my backyard because I couldn't imagine all the steps it would take to apply and get accepted and leave home and live in a dorm at a college outside Ravenna, Ohio.

I rode a bus six miles every day from Ravenna to Kent, not because Kent State University was a good, solid, affordable state school, which it was, but because I couldn't imagine how to make the leap and move away to college like my three older sisters and brother did. They went off to Ohio State University, one of the biggest colleges in the country. At Kent, my world stayed small and safe. I ate in the cafeteria with people from my high school.

A year or two into college, I flunked chemistry. It got too hard so I quit going to class. I changed my major three times. Then I got pregnant at 21 and dropped out of school. I quit drinking for good but stumbled through jobs that weren't right for me. A traffic clerk. A legal secretary. An office manager. A funeral home assistant picking up dead bodies.

What would I do with my life? The future overwhelmed me. Then one day a friend in recovery suggested this: just do the next right thing.

That's it?

I can do that.

Usually we know the next step to take but it's so small we don't see it because our vision is focused too far ahead and all we can see is a giant, scary leap instead of a small, simple step. So we wait. And wait. And wait, as if the Master Plan will be revealed in a massive blueprint rolled out like a red carpet at our feet.

Even if it were, we'd be too scared to step onto it.

I wanted to finish college, wanted a career I loved instead of a job I endured, but what should I major in? How would I pay for it? What job would it lead to? There were so many unanswered questions.

One day my mom revealed the next right step. "Just get a course catalog," she suggested.

That's it?

I can do that. So I got the catalog. Then I opened it up. Then I skimmed the pages with a highlighter and marked classes I'd like to take solely because they looked interesting, not because I had to earn a degree in something.

I sat on the floor in the living room flipping page after page. At first, like a kid whose favorite class is recess, I marked recreation classes, horseback riding, hiking and backpacking. Then a couple psychology and art classes. Then a slew of English classes. I turned every single page, reading every course description until I found a treasure trove. Newswriting. Reporting. Magazine writing. Feature writing. Wow. I went all the way from anthropology to zoology. Finished, flipped back, and looked at what courses got the most highlights.

Writing.

So I took one writing class. Then another. Then another.

When in doubt, do the next right thing. It's usually something quite small. As E. L. Doctorow said, writing a book is like driving a car at night. "You never see further than your headlights, but you can make the whole trip that way."

That philosophy applies to life, too. The headlights on my car shine 350 feet, but even with that much light, I can travel all the way to California. I need to see only enough light to get moving.

I graduated with a journalism degree from Kent State when I turned 30. Ten years later, I got my master's degree in religious studies from John Carroll University. I never set out to get a master's degree. If I had counted the years (five), the cost (thousands), and the time in the classroom, doing homework, doing research (late evenings, lunch hours, weekends), I never would have mailed that first tuition check.

I just took one class, then another and another, and one day I was done.

It was like that raising my daughter. I never dreamed I'd be a single parent for all 18 years of her childhood. My daughter finished high school the same month I got my master's degree. I'm glad I didn't know when I gave birth to her at 21 what it would cost in terms of time, money, and sacrifice to bring her to that graduation day. It would have terrified me.

Every so often some expert calculates how much it costs to raise a child. It's in the six-figure range. The money doesn't scare would-be parents away, but if someone calculated all the time and energy it took to raise a child, the human race would become extinct.

The secret to success, to parenting, to life, is to not count up the cost. Don't focus on all the steps it will take. Don't stare into the abyss at the giant leap it will take. That view will keep you from taking the next small step.

If you want to lose 40 pounds, you order salad instead of fries. If you want to be a better friend, you take the phone call instead of screening it. If you want to write a novel, you sit down and write a single paragraph.

It's scary to make major changes, but we usually have enough courage to take the next right step. One small step and then another. That's what it takes to raise a child, to get a degree, to write a book, to do whatever it is your heart desires.

What's your next right step? Whatever it is, take it.

Life Is Too Short to Waste Time Hating Anyone.

The children hadn't seen their dad in ten years.

Who could blame them?

They hadn't spoken to him in four years.

There was nothing left to say.

Their dad had never quit drinking. Like so many alcoholics, he would quit, but he always started again. He could get sober. He could never stay sober.

My friend Jane tried to make the marriage work despite the broken promises and empty bank account. She raised the kids; he raised the bottle.

For 20 years she stayed. He was a great guy when he wasn't drinking. He had a big heart and made them laugh. He wasn't abusive. He was guilty of neglect. He couldn't hold down a job. Couldn't pay the bills. Couldn't hold up his part of anything. They ended up losing their home for good.

Finally, one day Jane left what was left of the marriage. By the time they divorced in 1979, the kids were in their teens. The older daughter was 17, their son 15, and their younger girl 13. Years went by. Their dad floated in and out of their lives. He called the kids every few years. He tried rehab. He always relapsed.

Gradually, he faded completely from their lives. Ten years passed without a visit, four years without a call. Then the phone rang one spring. Someone from a Parma, Ohio, hospital phoned the son to locate the next of kin.

The son called his mom. Jane told me it felt as if someone had hit her in the stomach when she heard her son say, "Dad has terminal cancer."

But a strange thing happened. All the years of pain and anger vanished.

Her ex-husband had no money and no family. He'd never remarried. He'd never seen his six grandchildren. He was in bad shape. He'd been in the hospital for a week. He'd had an earlier surgery for colon cancer that they never knew about. He wouldn't last long.

She drove the kids to the hospital to see him. She didn't go in the room. Jane had remarried and built a new life. She hadn't seen her first husband in 20 years and didn't want to upset him by her presence, didn't want to upset herself and not be strong for the kids.

Sitting outside that room, she thought through what she had to do. On the drive home, she told the kids that she would pay for all the medical expenses. Then she helped get their dad into hospice. She went with the kids every day to visit him, to be their support, but she never stepped into his room. It wasn't her place to.

In the days he had left, he and the children came together as a family again. Resentments faded. When they talked about the past, they squeezed out memories of good times. They told him they loved him—and discovered they really did.

She and the kids planned the funeral, chose the casket, picked out the flowers. They decided there would be no wake. They didn't want to dishonor him by having hours pass with no visitors calling or with visitors who would ask too many questions about those lost years.

They wanted him to die in a way he didn't get to live—with dignity. When he passed away that June, they all found a new peace. They were free, and so was he. He would no longer suffer from cancer or from alcoholism.

One daughter read a poem she wrote. The others shared happy memories. My friend thanked everyone for coming. She paid for it all, the hospital bills, the hospice care, the funeral, the flowers.

When I asked why she went to such lengths to help a man who brought her so much pain, Jane said it was simple, "He was their father."

How do you get to that place of forgiveness and love?

It's pure grace for some, hard work for others.

For those who haven't received that grace, there's a blueprint for letting go of resentments in the "Big Book" of Alcoholics Anonymous. It's a solution that works for anyone willing to work it. The book says that a life which includes deep resentment leads only to futility and unhappiness. Resentments, it says, shut us off from the sunlight of the Spirit.

In the chapter "Freedom from Bondage," one person writes

about reading an article in a magazine written by a minister. This is what he says about resentments:

> If you have a resentment you want to be free of, if you will pray for the person or the thing that you resent, you will be free. If you will ask in prayer for everything you want for yourself to be given to them, you will be free. Ask for their health, their prosperity, their happiness, and you will be free. Even when you don't really want it for them, and your prayers are only words and you don't mean it, go ahead and do it anyway. Do it every day for two weeks and you will find you have come to mean it and to want it for them, and you will realize that where you used to feel bitterness and resentment and hatred, you now feel compassionate understanding and love.

I've tried it. The results are amazing.

Sometimes when I'm really stuck, I have to pray for the willingness to pray for the person. It always comes.

You want to be free of anger, hate, resentments? You set others free first. By setting her ex-husband free, Jane freed herself from the first part of her life and her children freed themselves for rest of their lives.

4

Don't Take Yourself So Seriously.
No One Else Does.

Lighten up. You're too intense. Don't take yourself so seriously.

I used to hear that all the time, from family, friends, coworkers, and any stranger who listened to me for more than five minutes.

What were they talking about? I had no clue until life wore me down and I surrendered. It took decades before I could wave the white flag and find peace in imperfection.

I was born with the idea that I had to be perfect in all things because deep down I felt like one big fat nothing at everything. All my life, my brain has sent out false warning signals. It constantly tells me that if I'm not perfect, I have failed. My brain is color-blind. It sees the world in black or white, yes or no, right or wrong, all or nothing. The gray matter between my ears can't discern that there are shades of gray coloring everything in life, that the world isn't a class you take pass-fail.

One day I finally understood that I was more high-strung than a dalmatian at a five-alarm fire. I had spent weeks working on a magazine story and it had just appeared in the Sunday newspaper. It had taken dozens of interviews and rewrites to get it perfect. Then the phone rang. One of the subjects thanked me for the article, but mentioned that I had spelled his name wrong. What?! I had double- and triple-checked every fact and spelling. Somehow one name had slipped by me.

I buried my face in my hands and wept at my desk. The story was more than 3,000 words long. I had spelled one single word incorrectly but I gave myself an F. When a coworker in the newsroom saw my tears, she rushed over. "Are you okay? What happened?" she asked, worried that someone had died.

"I...spelled...a...name...wrong," I gasped.

She looked at me shocked. "That's all?" she said. She shook her head and walked away. The look on her face stopped me dead. *Lighten up*, I heard. Only this time it wasn't anyone outside of me speaking. It came from inside of me.

Taking myself too seriously also turned me into a maniac multitasker. I couldn't delegate any task, no matter how small. They all had to be done just right, and only I knew the best way to complete them. I made endless to-do lists but forgot my own basic needs because the world couldn't turn without me. That's how important I was.

My houseplants were great indicators to prove my life and ego were out of control. The plants were like those caged canaries coal miners used to take down into the earth to tell when the air got bad. When the bird croaked, it was time to get out. When my plants were near death, it was a warning to come up for air, look at my life, and slow down my quest for perfection. If my plants were showing signs of neglect, I probably needed to spend more time with my daughter, too. Thank God, I never owned a pet.

There were a lot of signs telling me to lighten up, slow down, and focus on what really mattered. Like when I went to pick up a dirty glass and couldn't because it was stuck to the counter. Or when I ended up grocery shopping at the corner Dairy Mart because we were out of bread, milk, toilet paper, and Tang, which in my house was a staple. (My daughter used to pack the same sandwich almost every day—peanut butter on wheat bread with Tang sprinkled on it—a carryover from my youth.)

Being a single parent meant no one else was going to do the grocery shopping. If I didn't clear one evening or morning or weekend hour we ended up wiping with tissues instead of toilet paper, or worse.

In some areas I had already put on the brakes. I ate breakfast before leaving the house. I used to drive a stick shift while eating Cheerios. I had to get seat covers to hide the stains from falling food. I got a new car and a new rule: no eating or drinking behind the wheel. So far I'd broken it by eating solids but no liquids. (I tossed a newspaper on my lap to catch the crumbs.)

And I went the speed limit. A judge and two $50 fines within six weeks weren't enough to convince me years ago that it would be more economically feasible to leave my house ten minutes earlier than to drive 10 mph over the limit. It was when my car insurance went up that I vowed to obey the law. I take it as a compliment when people riding with me complain that I go too slowly.

I still get bruised every now and then from being in such a

hurry to live that elusive perfect life mapped out in my daily planner. My body is sometimes three steps behind my brain. I walk through a doorway too fast and bang my hips. I round a corner and forget my backside hasn't cleared it. File cabinets are the worst. The corners leave bruises that later turn a kaleidoscope of colors.

Those are nothing compared to the bruise my ego took one day when I was publicly humiliated for not taking the time to undress properly. I used to disrobe fast because I was in a rush to do something more important. I wouldn't take off my socks, pants, pantyhose, or underwear one at a time. I did it in one quick swoop. The panties and socks would end up somewhere buried in the pants.

I put on a pair of slacks in a hurry and rushed out the door. I was a comet of self-importance flying through the day. I had important things to get out of the way so I could get to more important matters. One of them was to buy a few groceries. When I stepped out of my car into the Sparkle Supermarket parking lot, my heel came down on something soft. At first I groaned, thinking it was dog doo. I looked down and saw a brown blob. It was a wad of women's hosiery. I reached down to pick it up and saw it was attached to something dangling from my pant leg.

Confused, I pulled and pulled and pulled, feeling something crawling up and down my leg until I was holding an entire pair of pantyhose in my hands. To my horror some man had been watching the retrieval from the sidewalk. That moment froze like a Kodak picture to remind me forever to lighten up and slow down.

I still bump into filing cabinets now and then, but so far the pantyhose incident has never been repeated. One time I did discover a lump on my thigh, reached into my jeans, and found a dirty sock left over from the last time I had worn it.

Maybe I should have left it there to cushion the bruises.

Pay Off Your Credit Cards Every Month.

My dad paid cash for everything.

If he didn't have the cash, he didn't need the item.

He was a sheet metal worker, roofer, and furnace repairman, depending upon the season. He hung spouting and repaired roofs in the summer; he made heating ductwork and fixed furnaces in the winter.

I never knew what he earned. What little he had, he spread over 11 kids. Suffice it to say, we didn't have many extras growing up, but we had everything we needed.

Dad never said, "We can't afford that." I never heard the words, "We don't have the money for that." He would look at what we wanted and say, "You don't need that." And he was right. Of course we didn't need it. We simply wanted it.

He taught us how to manage our wants.

I put off getting my first credit card until I needed one to make a hotel reservation. The card baffled me. No one had ever taught me anything about buying on credit. One time I paid the whole amount owed a week late. I figured paying the whole bill was smarter than paying the monthly minimum. On the next bill, I saw the $25 late fee. If I had paid less of the bill but paid it on time, it wouldn't have cost me $25. Lesson learned.

The interest part took longer to sink in. It took me a while to realize that the winter coat I bought on sale wasn't on sale if I was still paying for it six months later at 14 percent interest.

I started looking at everything itemized on that monthly bill. If I had paid cash for most of what was listed, I would have made different choices. It's easy to plunk down plastic on a $30 meal instead of shelling out three tens. Paying cash makes you think about skipping the appetizer and dessert. When I take actual money out of my wallet to pay $60 for a pair of jeans I want but don't need, I feel the hurt instantly and sometimes decide to put the jeans back. When I use a credit card, I don't feel any pain until the bill arrives. By then, it's a whopping hurt. By then, it's too late.

Most of us fritter away a dollar here, five dollars there. It adds up to hundreds or thousands every year. Many of us think, if only we earned more. If only we got a raise. If only we married money. I've watched Dr. Phil and Suze Orman enough to know that money problems are never about money. It's how you *think* about money. It's about how you *behave* with money. That, you can change.

By now most people have heard of the latte factor. In *The Finish Rich Workbook*, author David Bach writes that if you spend $3.50 every day on a latte, that's $24.50 a week. If you invested that with a 10 percent annual rate of return, you would have $242,916 in 30 years. I've never had a latte, but the concept can be applied to anything. I call mine the Oreo factor.

Saving 50 cents a day in loose change adds up to $15 a month. Cut soda pop consumption by one liter a week and you save $6 a month. Bring lunch to work, that's $60 a month. Eat out two fewer times a month, you save $30. Bounce one less check, that's $20. Pay credit card bills on time to avoid a late fee of $25. All that adds up to $1,872 a year.

I started jotting down how much I spent on junk food at vending machines, convenience stores, restaurants, coffee shops, and grocery stores. Potato chips, pop, candy bars, and cookies didn't seem to cost much until I added them up. It came to $30 a week. I couldn't believe it. The book convinced me to eat less junk and save the money I squandered on munchies.

It also convinced me to put a sticky note on my wallet that reads: *Pay cash. Wait 48 hours.* Before spending $100 on any nonemergency item, I wait two days to think about whether I really need or want it.

I no longer carry a credit card balance. Ever. If I buy something expensive and charge it, when I come home I write out a check for that amount to the credit card company. Some months I mail in four checks, but it doesn't hurt when I get the bill. I've already mentally — and physically — paid it.

Getting out of debt doesn't happen by winning the lottery. Ask all those folks who won it and squandered every dime. Getting out of debt starts with a change in your thinking, then a change in your behavior. It starts with small steps. It starts with separating your wants from your needs.

I once heard from a woman who kept every quarter she ever got to save $10,000 for her son's college tuition. Another woman saved 10 percent of everything she has ever earned, including Christmas and birthday gift money. When she was making only $5,800 a year, she saved $400 for a bedroom set.

One woman quit smoking. After nine years smoke-free, she bought central air, a new furnace, and carpeting with the $100 a month she saved. All that cash used to go up in smoke. Others have told me they save $10 a week in an account for Christmas or add up what they save using grocery store coupons. Another woman put a large glass container with a sign BEACH VACATION on it in the living room. When her children wanted money for ice cream or candy, she would remind them they could choose the candy or the vacation. By vacation time, they had half of what the trip cost. The kids learned a lesson in making good choices. Those kids were more disciplined than my husband and I. We tossed change in a five-gallon water cooler jug in our bedroom. It took us six years to fill it, but when we did, we had $1,300 to spend.

Living an abundant life doesn't mean winning the lottery, marrying rich, or getting a raise. It starts with a raise in consciousness and spreads from there. It starts with knowing that what you want isn't always what you need, and often isn't even what you truly want. It starts with making smart choices that lead to long-term gratification.

You Don't Have to Win Every Argument.
Agree to Disagree.

Before I got married, I laughed after reading about a couple who created a 16-page prenuptial agreement that detailed everything from not letting the car get lower than half a tank of gas to never leaving socks on the floor. Sixteen pages?

It wasn't so funny after I got married. When I bought a house with my spouse the ink on the purchase agreement was still wet when we hit major snags over minor details.

I always figured my mate for a diplomat. We got married late in life, the year I turned 40. Early on in the relationship when we were dating, Bruce once commented that there were two kinds of women: those who wear nail polish and those who don't. Which do you prefer? I asked, covering my hands. "Both," he said, not remembering which type I was.

His ability to say the right thing even when he's not sure what to say impressed me. Early on when we were dating, we hit a speed bump at a coffee shop that showed me what kind of guy he was. We were sitting outside at a table with his friend when an attractive woman bounced by with bountiful breasts unrestrained by a bra. The friend nudged my husband and they looked at her and grinned like teenagers. I was furious. After we left, we sat in the car and I told Bruce his behavior was rude to the woman and to me. I expected him to roll his eyes, tell me I was too sensitive and to get over it. I braced myself for an argument and ran through talking points in my head. Bruce listened to me, looked me in the eye, took my hand, and apologized right on the spot. "You're right," he said. "I acted like a teenager. I'll never do that again." What?! I wasn't prepared for that. I wanted to argue, wanted to press my points, wanted to win. Instead, he had surrendered.

He is one of the rare people I've met who, when he is wrong, promptly admits it with head held high, ego intact. He doesn't need to win every argument and is the first to admit when he can't. When he sees that the argument has reached an impasse, he calmly states like a Nobel Peace Prize winner, "You aren't going to convince me and I'm not going to convince you, so let's agree to disagree."

It's hard to argue with that.

I'd never heard of such a thing until I met him. At first I hated it when he turned into Mr. Mediator and used those words. To me, an argument always started with two sides and ended with one winner. And I had to be the winner. It could never end in a draw. Agree to disagree? That means no one has to be right and no one has to be wrong.

That's not easy, especially in a marriage. When we first learned our offer on the house was accepted, we both started planning how we would settle in. Instantly, I had the feeling we had bought two different houses. I figured we'd get rid of most of our collection of garage sale furniture and start over. He wanted to hang on to every ratty chair, couch, and lamp he had owned since college.

He figured my office would go in the second-floor room with the balcony. I wanted the room with the built-in bookshelves. He wanted to turn the breakfast nook into a computer kiosk. That was the quiet place I wanted to read the morning paper. He counted on buying a small washer and dryer and stacking them in the kitchen. I couldn't imagine smelling laundry soap while cooking spaghetti. He took one look at the side porch and imagined a screened-in sunroom. I took one look and saw a porch swing and plants.

Trying to play diplomat myself, I suggested we figure out what we would actually do in each room before we renovated. Hmmm. Let's see, kitchen and food. Kitchen and laundry. Which made more sense? Breakfast nook and computer, didn't sound like a match to me. He claimed the dining room for his wall of books. The place looked like a bookstore by the time he had unpacked.

He wanted to build shelves in the bathroom for a radio and TV (he watches CNN while he's shaving, even though he has a beard). He wanted the shelf to go right over the toilet and hold books and magazines. Books in the bathroom? How much time was he planning on spending in there?

If it's true that men are from Mars and women are from Venus, my husband is from Pluto. To me, a bedroom is the place you go to for refuge. To him, it's a den. In fact, he saw every room as a den. Since our house had no official den, he tried to turn every room into one. When he said den, I pictured dark paneling with duck wallpaper, a rack of guns, and assorted animal remains (deer head, stuffed shark, bear rug). He's not into carcasses, but he did need a place for all his gadgets big and small, including the $1,000 Crosstrainer machine, which he used twice, unless you count hanging clothes to air out. I call it the world's most expensive clothes rack.

Lest you think I'm inflexible, I had already compromised on the biggest thing: we agreed to use his bed, not mine. Right away, he claimed which side he wanted. Even when he lived alone, he always slept on the same side and kept the other side tucked in all night. He's a Virgo, so he's neat even in his sleep.

The big things were easier to compromise on than the small stuff. We ended up tripping over the little things, those speed bumps of life. He wanted to put up all 200 prints he had on the walls. He'd be happy if every room looked like a Friday's restaurant. I let him put his collection of Cold War memorabilia in the dining room. At least the fallout shelter signs, the yellow air raid horn, the giant tin of survival crackers, and the poster of a girl asking, "Mummy, what happens to us if the bomb drops?" made us feel grateful for every meal.

We ended up agreeing on everything except for the rest of his art prints, which stayed unhung, leaning against the walls for a year. I wanted one print per wall; he wanted them used like wallpaper. Finally, room by room, we agreed to disagree. He got his way on some walls; I got my way on others. We reached a stalemate when we came to the red racing cars framed in black. They looked like something a 15-year-old would hang over his bed—and take down once he turned 16.

I wanted to toss them out. He wanted to hang them in a prominent place.

"Can we agree to disagree?" I asked, trying out his Jimmy Carter routine. He finally agreed that we could store them in the basement until we could agree where to hang them. Three years later, he ran across them. "Whose are these?" he asked. He claimed he'd never seen them. We both had a good laugh, then hauled the prints out of the basement and agreed to agree: the racing car prints looked great — on the curb.

Cry with Someone. It's More Healing than Crying Alone.

I love going to movies. You can sit in the dark and weep away anonymously. Sometimes I cry over the film, sometimes over anything I've needed to cry about in the past few weeks. I use a good sad movie to catch up on all the tears I've stifled and held in too long.

Anyone who knows me well has seen me cry. My daughter teases me because I cry over Kodak commercials, over sappy TV dramas where you can predict the ending even before they cue the schmaltzy music.

All my life I've been a crier. Every day of grade school I cried about something. If an injustice was done to me or to anyone else, I cried. My siblings teased me for being a baby; so did my classmates and a few teachers. I couldn't help it. When I felt something, it came out my tear ducts. For years I tried to hold in the tears. My goal was to get through a whole day of grade school without crying. I finally did it—in the eighth grade.

I was in second grade when President John F. Kennedy died. The nuns at Immaculate Conception School held the First Lady up as a pillar of strength for not shedding a public tear. Jackie was the perfect widow, the perfect woman, the perfect Catholic. The world watched her in that black veil and saw a noble, dignified, and stoic widow who never broke down sobbing over his casket, not even when little John John saluted as it passed.

The nuns compared her to Mary, the mother of Jesus. They told us that Mary didn't cry. Not even when she stood at the foot of the cross. Not when she held her dead son. Not at his tomb. Never. For years I believed them.

Decades later, I read that Jackie Kennedy used to spend time alone on a friend's boat grieving over her husband's death. She waited until she was far out to sea, looked out over the vast ocean, and wept over how much she missed him. By the time I was done reading the article, I, too, was crying. How sad to have to hide your tears, especially tears of such deep sorrow.

I wonder what those nuns would say about her now. Come to think of it, I don't know if those nuns ever cried during my eight years of Catholic school. If they did, they never let us see it. Maybe tears were unholy under the old rules of the Church.

Many years after grade school ended, the movie *Jesus of Nazareth* came out. I loved the scene where Mary stands at the foot of the cross in the pouring rain, crying over the death of her son. She's not just crying, she's wailing and weeping. This

Mary weeps like a mother who has lost her son, not a saint bowing to God's most holy will. She weeps like all of us would want to but are afraid to.

Most of us were taught that tears are a sign of weakness. If you get upset at work, you go into the bathroom to cry. You hide in a stall and muffle the sobs with gobs of toilet tissue. Read any business article about how women can get ahead in the corporate world and they all warn: no tears. Don't ever let them see you cry.

If you cry out in the open, people try to stop you. It makes them uncomfortable. It's socially unacceptable. Worse than swearing. In fact, most people are more comfortable with someone swearing than crying. To cry openly shows a lack of control, a loss of power. In a culture that values strength, even tearing up is unacceptable.

All my life, I tried to become stronger by crying less. But whenever I held the sadness in, my face grew red, my cheeks hurt, and the tears escaped no matter how hard I tried to squeeze them back.

Then one day a counselor told me that those tears were an asset. Carol said they were part of me, just like my blue eyes and brown hair. "What a wonderful gift, to feel so intensely," she said.

The best advice I ever got on crying was to do it with someone. Carol told me that crying alone isn't as powerful as crying with another person. Cry alone and you'll keep crying those same tears over and over. Cry with someone and those tears have the power to heal you once and for all.

When I was getting my master's degree in religious studies, I read a book about a saint who nearly lost his vision because he cried so much and so often. Saint Ignatius, who founded the Jesuits, considered his tears to be a great gift from God. He inspired me to write a 22-page paper on the gift of tears.

Ignatius was a macho military man bent on knighthood and the pursuit of happiness through women and power until a cannonball shattered his leg and he found God. He mentions tears 175 times in the first part of his spiritual diary and speaks of tears in every single entry in the second half. They weren't a few drops here and there, but great torrents so intense they left him speechless. Those tears brought him great gifts — humility, intimacy with God, greater devotion, peace, and strength. He considered tears to be a mystical grace.

Too bad so many men and women refuse to cry and boast of not doing it. I remember someone telling me after seeing the movie *Schindler's List* that he almost cried. Almost? Why did he hold back?

Why did Jackie? Or the nuns? Why does anyone? I couldn't even if I wanted to. I let the tears flow and make sure all my mascara is waterproof.

One of my favorite verses in the Christian Bible is the shortest one of all: "Jesus wept." He showed his humanity. He shed messy, unmanly tears. He didn't do it in private. He did it in front of his friends and followers. In front of a crowd.

We need to stop hiding our tears and actually share them. It takes a strong person to cry. It takes a stronger person to let others see those tears. We need to be tough enough to be tender, no matter who is watching.

It's Okay to Get Angry with God.
He Can Take It.

When was the last time you got angry with God?

We're not supposed to get mad at God, right?

He'll send hellfire and brimstone.

Hellfire I can picture, but what exactly is brimstone?

Growing up Catholic I never heard any priest grant us permission to rage against God. Our job was to fear God; God's job was to scare us.

There's an old story about a rabbi who sends his disciples out the day before Yom Kippur to learn from a tailor how to approach the Day of Atonement. In the ten days between the Jewish New Year—Rosh Hashanah and Yom Kippur—religious Jews undertake spiritual housecleaning. Yom Kippur is the holiest day of prayer, a time for fasting and reflection. They examine the previous year, make amends, and commit to doing better.

As the disciples spy on the tailor, they see him remove a

book from his shelf. Inside is a list of all the sins he committed through the year. Then the tailor tells God it is time to settle their account. He holds up the book and offers the list of his sins.

Then the tailor takes down another book. Inside are all the sins God committed, the pain, the grief, the heartache God sent the tailor and his family. The tailor tells God, "Lord of the Universe, if we were to total the accounts exactly, You would owe me much more than I would owe You."

Pretty bold, don't you think?

Instead of haggling with God over what's in the book, the tailor seeks peace. He makes a deal with God that he'll forgive God His sins if God will forgive him his. The man pours himself a glass of wine, blesses it, and says, "Let there now be peace and joy between us. We have forgiven each other. Our sins are now as if they never were."

A clean slate with God. A clean slate for God.

We could all use a period of amnesty with God. How many people turn away from God or hold a grudge because of the pain, grief, and heartache in our lives?

How many people question where God was...when the planes crashed into the Twin Towers...when a son died of leukemia, when a daughter committed suicide, when we felt unbearable despair and loneliness?

No one really has the answer. We're all guessing. The standard line of preachers is that God has given us free will and won't intervene in the day-to-day workings of our lives. Even if we beg? Those same preachers tell us that God blesses us with our children, jobs, talents, et cetera. If God can give gifts, can't God withhold all those things we don't want? Why doesn't God protect us from disease, death, and destruction?

I don't always understand how God works, but I still pray. It's like that old saying, I don't understand how electricity works, either, but I don't let that keep me in the dark. I don't have to understand God to believe in God. What gives me hope are those words some anonymous soul wrote: "I believe in the sun, even when it is not shining. I believe in love, even when I feel it not. I believe in God even when He is silent."

I've had my share of feeling abandoned by God. It took years of counseling to cleanse me from the residue of childhood that left me feeling bruised and battered. Near the end of therapy, after I had spent months dealing with all the characters involved, my counselor suggested there was one main player left. She told me it was okay to get angry with God for not rescuing me, for not being there when I needed someone to protect me.

Nope. I'm not mad at God, I told her. But underneath my faith was a deep well of doubt that nagged and taunted, "Where was God? I wouldn't let a child suffer. How could God?"

Shhh, I silenced it. God was always there, I lied. No way was I going to risk getting angry with God. Not when God was all I had to cling to some days. How could I get angry with God? How dare I?

I never forgot those pictures in first grade at Immaculate Conception. The Baltimore Catechism that showed how black the soul looked when you sinned. Wouldn't getting angry with God be the darkest sin of all? It would fall into the mortal sin category and tip the scales on the ledger God kept on me and my soul.

There would be no sky turning black, no bolts of lightning striking me dead, no voice booming out like thunder to condemn me. I wasn't that naive. It wasn't lightning I feared. It was losing my job or my health or my daughter. I wasn't going to fail the Job test. The famous biblical character was tempted to blame God for causing his terrible troubles. So I prayed and pretended everything was fine. Yep, everything was great with God. It was the rest of the world and everyone in it that got on my last nerve.

One day at work I blew up at my boss over something so trivial I can't remember it. I stormed out of the newsroom, hopped in my car, and screeched my tires as I peeled out of the parking deck. Thank God my boss wasn't walking across the parking lot because I might not have hit my brakes. I got home and stuffed the rage building inside me and sat down with my sewing machine to calmly repair a dress. Halfway through, the needle on the machine broke in half.

That's when I snapped.

I pounded my fists. I swore. I got in my car and went for a drive. I screamed all my hate and rage at all the people who had abandoned me and hurt me. When I was done I realized it wasn't my boss or my dad or my mom or the nuns or any other authority figure from my past. It was the number one guy who pissed me off. I took the rest out on God. I cursed God up and down and even dropped the F-bomb. Suddenly, I felt something strange come over me.

Peace.

Underneath all that anger was the deepest calm.

Underneath that pile of resentments was God's love.

I felt an inner glow warm me, as if God was smiling on

me saying, "Now, don't you feel a whole lot better?" I started to laugh. God wanted me to unload the dump truck I'd been driving around for years so we could get closer.

A Jesuit priest put a name on that prayer. I met Father Jim Lewis at the Jesuit Retreat House in Parma. He was profound in his simplicity. He told me that God wants a real, authentic, genuine relationship with us, the same kind of openness and honesty you have in a good marriage.

He discovered that after struggling with a job transfer. He hated his new assignment. He tried holy obedience and acceptance, but he was miserable. He tried to pray with gratitude but didn't have any in him. He tried to play God's happy little servant, but it wasn't working.

Finally, one day he broke. He went to the chapel alone, greeted God then softly cursed his holy heart out. "Damn. Damn. Damn. Damn. Damn." That was it. He said the same prayer every day until it was out of his system. Once the anger was gone, there was room for something else. Peace. The slate was clean. Now God could write on it.

Father Lewis called it the Damn Prayer.

It's a great prayer to use when you're all bottled up.

God doesn't want us to be so holy we aren't human. God doesn't want fake prayers and phony praise. God wants an honest, genuine, real relationship.

God and I are best buds now. Every evening, we take a walk. Every morning, we sit together in silence. All through the day we chat. Well, I do most of the talking. No matter what happens or doesn't during the day, we go to bed with a clean slate. As in a good marriage, nobody goes to bed angry.

The Most Important Sex Organ
Is the Brain.

M^y friend Sheryl wanted me to meet her friend.

I don't do fix ups, I told her.

It's just a party, she said.

She didn't tell me much about the guy. He had a beard, he was divorced, he was in public relations. That's it.

Had she told me more, that he smoked, that he was an agnostic who loved jazz and sushi and big city life, that he was a Virgo who was never home, I would have never given him a chance. I was a nonsmoking Catholic vegetarian Gemini who loved country music and small towns and nesting most nights. On paper, we were no match.

At the last minute, I decided to go to that party back in 1992. Sheryl introduced me to Bruce and we never stopped talking. We sat on the couch for hours. He loved his work and was passionate about making a difference in the world. He had beautiful warm brown eyes that made me feel safe, yet they were alive with excitement. There was something going on behind those eyes.

He called the next day and we talked for three hours. I learned that he sang in the shower and cried at movies. But I was cautious. I had given up on men for a while, stayed celibate for almost two years. After a few years of intense counseling to deal with childhood issues, I wanted to break the pattern of attracting unavailable men who struggled with intimacy and commitment. I wanted someone to love me, to want me for the long haul. Like every wounded woman, I wanted someone who would never hurt me, never let me down, never reject or abandon me. It was an impossible order.

I didn't know what to do with Bruce, so on our first real date, I gave him three choices: we could see a movie, go out for dinner, or drive to the town he grew up in and do a tour of his homes, school, and points of interest so I could learn more about him. He turned the tables on me and suggested we do the tour in my hometown.

We drove around Ravenna, population 12,000. We drove past my grade school, junior high, high school, places I worked, my old home, and my church. We ended up at the cemetery where my grandparents are buried. We sat in the car watching a fingernail clipping of a moon rise over the scarlet sky and naked trees. He declared that moment with me was as good as sex. This man was certainly different from anyone I'd been with.

Later that night, we ended up at a restaurant talking about what we were looking for. Would he ever marry again? Would I ever marry at all? We agreed on one thing: if we did, we would choose not a husband or wife, but a life partner, a best friend.

That night I started to trust loving a man. Bruce was bright, funny, and honest. I learned he was Jewish but loves to sing Christmas carols outside cafés in December. That he gives the Little Rascals high sign to kids, has tons of books in his living room, and would quit smoking for the right person.

He loved my wild wavy hair, my skinny nose, my hands, my freckles. He showed me pictures of his mom, grandma, sons, and siblings. He even took out his cell phone, turned it off, and said, "I never do this." He mailed me a cassette tape of romance and jazz on one side and his favorite Christmas songs on the other. He said he sent it to seduce me. It worked.

All his words and acts of kindness made me feel safe. He acted like a child, so happy to see me. He held my hand and we sat talking on the couch for hours. It was like having a sleep-over with a best friend. Bruce became my buddy.

We didn't have sex until we had The Talk. His idea, not mine. One night we sat up all night on the couch talking. He wanted to know about my past relationships, all the detours and broken roads that led me to him. He'd been married for 15 years, divorced for two. I had never lasted more than a year with the same guy. Lots of dad issues, lots of men who resembled my dad and brought their mother issues. Not a good combination. Bruce joked that he liked a woman with a past. We laughed but we also cried as I talked and he listened to the challenges of loving me. There was still so much healing to be done. In my entire life, I'd never felt completely emotionally and physically safe with a man. I was barely aware of my own intimacy needs. I grew up believing that a woman performed for a man and if she got something out of it, fine, but if not, it didn't matter.

Bruce encouraged me to speak up about everything, to say what I liked and didn't. I didn't know what I liked or wanted in a relationship because I never got the chance to figure it out. Most people emerge into a sexual being. When you are abused sexually as a child or raped as a teenager as I was, your sexual identity is stolen. You don't get to gradually come of age. When someone else's sexuality is forced on you, it stunts your own growth. I spent my adult life trying to please a man by doing all the things I guessed he wanted, but didn't have a clue as to what made me feel good.

Bruce wouldn't have that. He told me the key to our relationship was building and keeping a friendship, that sex wouldn't make or break a relationship. He taught me a great eternal truth: friendship comes first. That is the soul of the relationship, he said.

Before I met Bruce, a girlfriend in recovery had shared how she created new ways to relate to men by using the "Big Book" of Alcoholics Anonymous. The writers of it must have had a sense of humor, because the sex advice starts on page 69. The book advises one to take a personal inventory, to look at resentments and fears, but also at one's sex life, what worked and what didn't. Then create a sane and sound ideal between you and God about what is right for you alone.

I needed to trust God with my sexuality. I had to look at sex as a gift that springs from a God who made me with desires and longings and passions. I needed to know and believe that God was creative enough to design men who would not abuse or abandon me in a relationship.

Sex had to be part of a larger, whole relationship. This time, it was. Before we ever got to "home plate" we sat and talked for hours. At one point, Bruce pointed to his head and said, "Sex is up here." It's not about performing for each other. It's not your job to please anyone. "Not that much of sex is about having an orgasm," he said. "That's the icing. All the other ingredients make up the cake. Let's make the cake."

So we did. A decade later, we're still having a great time baking. Our sex life has never been dependent on our bodies alone. Good thing, because age comes along and changes them. In my case, cancer did. After I lost my breasts to cancer, it took a while to feel sexy again. Bruce kept telling me it would just take a little time for my brain to rewire itself. He was right.

When it comes to sex, the most important erogenous zone is between your right ear and your left ear.

10

God Never Gives Us More than We Were Designed to Carry.

There's a lovely line in the book *Breath, Eyes, Memory* that makes you look differently at the things we carry, the problems we resent, the gifts we envy.

Author Edwidge Danticat describes a group of people in Guinea who carry the sky on their heads. In her lyrical novel about the tragedy and trauma one family of women face, she tells the tale of a people who are powerful enough to bear all things. Their Creator designed them to carry more than others. They don't know that they were chosen for this. But if you experience many difficulties in life, you were designed to bear them.

Some of us are asked to bear more than others. My uncle Paul was chosen to carry part of the sky.

He and my aunt Veronica were my godparents. They had five children when their last child was born. When we got the news, we cried. The good news was they had a baby boy. The bad news was, he had something wrong with him.

Brett Francis Kelly was born back in 1972, when people used words like *Mongoloid* and *retard*. It was a time when relatives whispered the bad news through tears, when doctors suggested institutional care, when support for special needs children didn't exist.

Brett wasn't the perfect healthy baby every parent prays for. He had ten fingers and ten toes, but he also had something else. My cousin was born with an extra 21st chromosome. He had Down syndrome. Back then, children with Down syndrome weren't considered special. They were considered disasters. But my aunt and uncle loved him the same as their other five.

Then my aunt got cancer. The breast cancer spread to her bones. She died when Brett was only three. She left my uncle a widower with six children. How could my uncle Paul raise six children alone? The oldest was only 14.

It got worse. Uncle Paul got fired from his job. He had missed too much work caring for his sick wife. There was no Family Leave Act to protect him. What happened to the family? My uncle held them together. He made Brett the center of their universe. That broken piece somehow made them whole.

Uncle Paul never complained about being a single parent of six. He got a real estate license so he could work from home. He did the laundry and cleaned the house after the kids went to bed. He never remarried. He always said, "I married for life." He made Brett his life partner. The two were inseparable.

Brett had no edit button. If he thought something, he said it. He couldn't lie. When he saw a woman with a large derriere, he would announce, "You have a big butt." When he caught the reflection of his fuller-than-full figure, he'd tell the mirror, "I'm so sexy" and believed it.

Brett left his imprint everywhere. At my cousin Bridget's wedding, he pretended to be the bartender. At my brother Jim's wedding, he gyrated on the dance floor until his pants nearly fell off. At my uncle John's funeral, he spilled water on himself and took off his pants and ended up wrapped in a blanket.

He never grew up. That was the joy of Brett. He stayed a child. He also stayed his dad's best buddy. The decades flew by. Each child played mom, then went off to college and passed the role on to the next younger sibling.

When my uncle turned 80, we wondered who would take Brett one day. The problem wasn't that Brett would be a burden no one wanted to bear. The problem was that all his siblings wanted him to move in with them.

It wasn't long after my uncle turned 80 that we got the bad news.

The day before Brett's sister was to marry, the family had gathered for the rehearsal dinner. They had spent the entire day together, all the sisters and brothers and in-laws and grandkids and Uncle Paul. At one point, out of the blue, Brett told them, "Don't worry. Mom's here. Everything's going to be fine."

After dinner, Brett collapsed from a pulmonary embolism. No one could revive him.

The funeral home overflowed with photos. Brett in his First Communion jacket. Brett in a cap and gown. Brett in his basketball uniform. Brett with his Special Olympics medals. My uncle had made sure Brett's life was a rich one.

At the funeral Mass, the priest asked us to examine how we

use our gifts. Brett came by his gifts naturally, the priest said. They came with that extra chromosome.

"We need the Bretts of this world," he said in his sermon. "Brett wasn't handicapped. He showed us what God expects from us: to celebrate every time we take a breath."

We need the Uncle Pauls of the world, too. It was his quiet strength that held up the world so Brett could skip through it, so Brett could celebrate everything as only Brett could. In his world, the Easter Bunny and Santa Claus were real, birthdays lasted seven days, and there was no such thing as race, only people with better tans.

My uncle smiled as his son Paul gave the eulogy. "People always told us we were a great gift to Brett," Paul said. "It was the other way around. He was a great gift to us."

Uncle Paul made it so by holding the family together, by holding up the sky above them.

My uncle called one random day just to tell me how proud he is of me. I saved the message and replay it to hear his voice, shaky from Parkinson's and age, still full of sweet gratitude. Uncle Paul never lamented the life he was given.

He'd be the first to say God never gives us more than we were designed to carry. Some of us were designed for more, some for less. No matter what, even if we are asked to carry a portion of sky, it is beyond bearable. It is gift.

11

Make Peace with Your Past So It Doesn't Screw Up the Present.

Ever have one of those days where everything is fine and then suddenly it isn't?

Nothing on the outside has changed, but everything inside you just did. Something you can't name happened, and suddenly, you find yourself at the bottom of a hole deep inside yourself.

It's hard to figure out what sent you spiraling down. A noise. A smell. A comment. Something so small sends you back into your own personal darkness, fear, and despair. It happens so fast, you don't know how you got there. Or sometimes you can feel yourself falling in slow motion but you can't stop it.

What sets it off? It's different for everybody, especially those who have suffered child abuse or neglect in some form or another. For me, something as small as the smell of chalk and milk cartons will do it. The sight of tiny folding chairs like those we had in first grade. The sound of a weeping child in a store. The sight of an angry parent dragging a toddler across a parking lot. The sound of flesh hitting flesh in a violent movie.

Some days, any one of those sends me into the hole. All at once, I feel scared and lonely and disconnected. I call them attacks of childhood. In a flash, I'm suddenly not a full-functioning adult. I'm powerless and scared and can't figure out why. One therapist who used to counsel Vietnam veterans told me that adults who suffered abuse and neglect as children can have post-traumatic stress. Childhood injuries remain with us for years. Like shrapnel, the pieces keep working their way out of the body.

It used to take me days to climb out of the hole. Meanwhile, I'd go to work, fix dinner, play with my child, try to function, but inside it felt like I was on the verge of an emotional breakdown. If someone pulled one more string, I'd unravel in a puddle of yarn and no longer be whole.

We all have childhood holes. Most people have a few here and there that are small enough to avoid and easy to get out of quickly. Others have a lunar landscape of deep craters left behind from mentally ill relatives or teachers, encounters with domestic violence and sexual abuse, or beatings and rages by parents who were also once children who were abused or neglected by someone else.

Big things rarely push you in the hole. Big things you can see coming and avoid. If you see or hear a train coming, you step off the tracks and stay out of the way. It's the small things that knock you down the hole. Things you don't see coming until you look in the rearview mirror.

One day I pulled my car into the garage as I do every day. My husband was standing in the driveway and told me to move my car up an inch. So I did. It still wasn't good enough for him. No, a little more, he insisted. I could have easily smiled and moved it up or left it alone or handed him the keys to park it perfectly. Instead, I felt an instant rage come over me, like he'd lit a short fuse to a huge bomb. KABOOM! I was blasted back to childhood. Why do I have to be perfect? Why am I never good enough? Why do I even bother?

But instead of exploding, I usually implode. Instead of yelling and raging, I cave in and cry. They're old tears. I can feel them come from a different place in me. My face hurts, my sinuses ache, and afterward, I need to sleep.

The incident with the car? Hours later, I was able to trace it back in time to the exact moment it triggered, decades earlier when I was 21. I'm standing in my parents' driveway and my dad wants me to help him put a TV in the back of his station wagon. It's heavy and awkward and I'm not sure how he expects me to carry it and squeeze it into the small spot he pointed to. I grab my half of the TV and slide it in the car. He tells me to move it back. Back where? I don't know what he wants. He screams at me. My dad was either quiet or screaming. I don't know why, but he'd go from zero to 100 in a flash. His rages were almost always accompanied by these words: "What the hell's wrong with you? Can't you do anything right?"

Standing there in the driveway holding the TV, he screamed them. I couldn't drop it and leave so I was stuck standing there as a target for his anger. There was never an apology, never an acknowledgment that he was having a bad day or a bad moment.

Over time I learned how to get unstuck. First, you have to recognize that you're stuck. For me here's my warning sign: whenever my emotions don't match what just happened, it's about my childhood. I've learned to freeze the moment, just like you would pause a movie, and ask: Wait. Is this reaction about the present moment? Or is it about the past? I can't change the past. But by changing my response to its leftovers, I can change the present.

One counselor helped me avoid falling in the hole by using this technique. Get an index card. Jot down proof that you are a functioning adult. Write down your age, education level, degrees, job title, the fact that you can drive a car, parent, vote, and other things adults do. When you find yourself teetering over a hole, take out the card and read it. Get grounded in today, in the adult you are, not the kid you were. It helps you regain your footing.

On the other side of the card, write down your search and rescue team. List your 911 friends to call to help you get out of the hole. Choose people in your inner circle, people who love you the most, as is. People who aren't afraid to search in the dark for you, people who can yank you back into the light.

It takes work to rewire your thoughts about yourself, but when you do, everything in your life changes for the better — especially your most intimate relationships. If you don't do the hard work, you will constantly bump into your past and run into the worst of your mom and dad in every relationship. Rewiring your thoughts won't get rid of the holes in life, but it can prevent you from falling in them.

My friends in recovery told me this story:

A drunk leaves the bar one night and on his way home

stumbles and falls into a deep hole in the road. He can't get out. One passerby tosses him a Bible, cites a Scripture passage to give him hope, and leaves. A counselor stops and tries to help him figure out why he fell in the hole. Finally, a recovering alcoholic hears the screams and stops. "Can you help, please?" the man in the hole cries. "Sure," the sober man says. He jumps into the hole. The alcoholic screams. "Oh, no, now we're *both* stuck in this hole!" The sober man smiles and says, "Don't worry. I've been here before. I know my way out. We climb out together."

The goal isn't to walk around the hole. Or get out quicker. The goal is to fill the hole so no one else falls in it. What do you fill it with? God. Which is to say, love: love of self, love of others, love of God.

The last time I climbed out of the "I'm not enough" hole, I prayed, "How will I ever believe that I'm good enough?" The answer came in that small still voice from my heart: "By helping others believe that *they* are good enough."

It's Okay to Let Your Children See You Cry.

My dad wasn't much of a crier.

In the 42 years I knew him, I remember seeing him cry only twice. First, when his youngest sister died of cancer. The other time, after he got angry and kicked my brother out of the house.

He regretted that decision the moment my brother closed the door and drove off. Dad moped around for weeks, then finally, with tears in his eyes, asked me to talk my brother into returning.

Dad wasn't allowed to cry growing up. Life was too tough for tears. He had to be tougher. He survived the Great Depression but the family farm didn't. He watched the farm he loved slip from his own dad's grasp. They ran out of money, then ran out of luck. My dad got yelled at for feeding extra oats to the horses, which would surely have died of starvation if he hadn't. He quit school in eighth grade to go to work to help the family survive.

He wasn't big on tears. Whenever we cried, he'd holler at us, "What are you crying about? I'll give you something to cry about." It just made me cry more. Too many men grow up without shedding a tear. I once read an article about baseball great Pete Rose tearing up over some sports achievement he had finally reached. He told the press it was the first time he had cried. The first time? He was already a father himself. Hadn't he cried over the birth of his own child?

There's something special about letting your kids see you cry. It doesn't mean you're weak. It means you are human. It lets them know they're allowed to feel life deeply and fully. I'll never forget the dad who called me once to share the best basketball game he'd ever seen, one that left him in tears, tears he was glad his son got to see.

LeBron James was playing ball that night. The Chosen One had an entourage and national press coverage that followed him everywhere, even back in high school. He drove a Hummer and had million-dollar sneaker deals in his grasp before he joined the NBA.

Like so many dads, this one wanted his son to see LeBron play, so they arrived at the high school gym early to get a good seat. LeBron was the best high school player anyone had seen in years. He would soon be snatched up by the pros, but for now, he was playing for his high school, St. Vincent-St. Mary in Akron.

The dad and his son sat in the bleachers waiting for the Wadsworth High School junior varsity game to end. Suddenly, with one minute left on the clock, the JV game came to a halt.

Wadsworth was winning by 10 points when the Cloverleaf High School coach stopped the game. The crowd buzzed, wondering why the coach called a time-out when the game wasn't close enough to win, when everyone was anxious for the real game to begin, the game that mattered, the game with LeBron.

That's when the dad noticed the short, skinny player sitting at the end of the bench wearing the green No. 10 jersey for the Cloverleaf Colts. When the player rose from the bench, the dad noticed the boy's limp, the slight tilt of his head, the way his eyes looked a tad off, the scarred ear that had never finished growing in the womb.

The dad didn't know that a shunt in the boy's head kept him alive, drained the water from his brain, and kept him from playing sports to the fullest. The boy couldn't afford to be hit in the head. Doctor's orders.

The coach had planned to put Adam Cerny into the game, no matter how close the score. He knew how badly Adam wanted to play against the school's big rival and figured Adam had earned the right to play. Adam was the first to arrive for every practice and the last to leave. He cleaned the floor, lugged water bottles, and got the basketballs out.

The dad and boy in the bleachers watched as Adam caught a pass and launched a shot from well beyond the three-point line. He missed.

Instead of pouncing all over the ball to charge down the court and rack up more points, the teenagers on the opposing team didn't move. They wanted Adam to have another chance.

The clock ticked down. Adam shot and missed. Twelve

seconds. He missed again. And again. Ten seconds. Nine seconds. The Wadsworth team refused to take the ball. One player even motioned for Adam to come closer, but the boy declined.

By now, everyone was standing and cheering for Adam Cerny. The people who knew him shouted, "Come on, Adam!" and "Cer-nee! Cer-nee!" With four seconds left, Adam launched the ball. The buzzer split the air as the ball swooshed through the net.

The crowd went wild.

Fans from both teams stood to cheer and clap. The Wadsworth players shook his hand and patted his back. The two referees on the gym floor applauded. One turned to the other and said, over and over, "Man, was that nice."

The dad in the stands began to cry. He cried over what high school basketball had become in a different arena, with autograph seekers, TV crews, and security guards hovering around a teenager who had legal teams ready to negotiate tennis-shoe deals in the millions for a boy dubbed King James who would skip college and head straight to the NBA.

The dad cried over seeing a three-pointer that was better than any pro, college, or high school game he'd ever watched. His eyes filled and tears fell. When he looked up, his son, a child of five, asked if the tears were because Cloverleaf had lost the game. The dad couldn't explain. He just smiled and hugged his son tight.

What a gift that father gave his son. I hope that boy will remember those tears. I hope his dad will tell him the story of what caused them and give them both something to cry about.

Don't Compare Your Life to Others'. You Have No Idea What Their Journey Is All About.

On Vocations Day at school, I always ducked.

The principal at Immaculate Conception School would announce that Father So-and-So was going to talk to us about choosing a vocation. There were only two choices: to become a nun or a priest.

I dreaded The Talk. The priest paced the room, scanning our faces for halos. He told us some boys and girls in this room had a vocation, a calling to do something special with their lives.

I would slide behind the kid in front of me so the priest wouldn't choose me, and neither would God. If God didn't see me, He wouldn't pick me. I didn't want to wear a habit and tuck my hair into that contraption the Dominicans wore on their heads that left only a face showing.

On recruitment day, the choices were simple: choose God

or choose the world. The only way to serve God completely was to be in a religious order. There were so many to choose from: Franciscan, Jesuit, or Maryknoll priests; Ursuline, Dominican, or Incarnate Word nuns. They even had brochures to attract recruits, like the army.

As far as I know, no one in my class got the calling. We went on to choose normal jobs and lives, to date, to marry, to have children, and not always in that order. I sometimes wondered whether we were choosing second best, choosing the world over God. We didn't have vocations and callings; we opted for jobs and careers.

It took years for me to understand the concept of vocation. That we each had one and the choices weren't limited to religious orders. And that we weren't supposed to compare them and measure them against anyone else's.

We are all in this world for something greater than self. We each have a mission, an assignment, a calling, a vocation that is ours and ours alone. The best description I ever read of vocation is by writer and theologian Frederick Buechner. It helped me to fine-tune my focus in life. To paraphrase Buechner, the place God chose for you is the intersection where your greatest joy and the world's greatest need meet.

For years I struggled to find mine. I wanted a life of meaning and purpose. I stumbled on a broken path full of potholes and detours and orange construction barrels. I worked as a cashier dusting vitamins at a pharmacy. Then as a waitress. I wore a pink uniform and hairnet as a dietary worker at a hospital, putting prune whip on patients' trays. I gave first aid as an emergency medical technician. I picked up corpses for a funeral home. I collected speeding ticket fines and filled in dockets as a court clerk. I typed up legal briefs as a secretary for the county public defender. I ran the front desk of an outpatient alcoholism treatment center. I counseled alcoholics and ran group therapy.

It took decades to end up as a writer doing what I love. All the time I looked around me comparing my insides to everyone else's outsides. I wanted what others had simply because I didn't have it. They all had it so much easier, I whined. I wanted their lives. They looked so much better than mine.

I stopped whining the day my fiancé cheated on me and I handed back the ring. A man is not a financial plan, I finally realized. My future was up to me. That's when I went back to college and pursued my dream to be a writer.

In time, I found out that in God's economy nothing is ever wasted. All those "dead-end jobs" prepared me for the job of my dreams in journalism. Being an EMT taught me to work on deadline. Picking up dead bodies taught me how to talk to grieving families. Working in the court system taught me how to read legal briefs and research criminal records for stories. Counseling alcoholics taught me interviewing and listening skills that helped me develop the bullshit detector every reporter needs.

All my jobs prepared me for my life's assignment.

I love to tell people I haven't worked since 1986. I get paid to write. To write! My vocation is to inspire people through writing. That is the place where my deep gladness and the world's deep hunger meet. I write to make people feel less alone.

What is your deep gladness? Where does it meet the world's deep hunger? Does it at all? That's what you need to discover.

People who don't know my journey will say, "You're so

lucky." Luck? Grace, I'll credit, but not luck. You can compare yourself to those above you and whine or compare yourself to those below you and gloat, or you can stay focused on that man or woman in the mirror and embrace his or her unique assignment with gratitude.

What is your assignment here?

You can be anything—a doctor, lawyer, social worker, mayor, president, columnist—but why not find out what you are called to be?

It doesn't matter what has happened to you, it matters what you do with what has happened to you. Life is like a poker game. You don't get to choose the cards you are dealt, but it's entirely up to you how to play the hand. One of my favorite lines in the movie *Harry Potter and the Chamber of Secrets* is when the great sage Dumbledore tells Harry, "It is not our abilities that show what we truly are. It is our choices."

Choice, not chance, determines your destiny. It's up to you to decide what you are worth, how you matter, and how you make meaning in the world. No one else has your gifts—your set of talents, ideas, interests. You are an original. A masterpiece.

Show the world the miracle you were created to be. Fake it till you make it. We're all faking it. The greatest writers wake up every day gripped by fear that they'll never write another interesting word. The greatest business leaders wake up wondering whether today is the day the world will find out what great phonies they really are. The greatest religious leaders struggle daily with faith. The greatest political leaders worry that each decision will cost them the next election.

No one feels completely confident or secure. We get mere

moments of that. We're all afraid of making *the* mistake that will ruin our lives. There's probably no such thing. Even if we made every mistake we feared would ruin us, our lives wouldn't be ruined. They would be changed.

We're all scared that we're doing it wrong, that people don't like us, that we'll never be smart enough, good enough, successful enough, attractive enough. Don't fight it. Make it roller-coaster scary. Enjoy the bumps, the wild turns, the ups, the downs, the almost-lost-my-lunch lurches. Life will kick you around like a World Cup soccer ball. Keep your bounce. Enjoy the ride. Fear and excitement are best friends. Stay in good company.

Don't try to fill anyone else's shoes. The world doesn't need you to be Mother Teresa, Gandhi, Martin Luther King, Michael Jordan, Maya Angelou, or Bill Gates. The world needs you to be you.

14

If a Relationship Has to Be Kept Secret, You Shouldn't Be in It.

In my twenties and thirties I went through men like bread crumbs through a goose. The truth is, I kept dating the same man, he just came with different names.

I never realized it until one relationship landed me in therapy. The young, handsome guy who hit on me at work seemed thrilled to be dating me. He gushed over me for about three months. Just when I was ready to let down my guard, he told me he couldn't go out with me that weekend because his fiancée was coming to town.

His what?!

Yep. He was engaged. I was, once again, someone's secret side dish. I was furious. I had done my homework. The guy wasn't gay, married, or addicted to anything. So how was it, once again, I found myself dating a man who wasn't free?

Story of my life. Why did I keep repeating this story? The

night I told him to get lost, I cried and prayed and yelled to the universe, "Why do I keep attracting men who aren't available?"

The universe answered, "Because you're afraid of ones who are."

Whoa. I realized that I was scared of a man who might stay. Why? I grew up with a man in the house who ranted and raved and raged. On the flip side, he was the most generous, giving, selfless dad you ever met. But you never knew which side you were going to get. Somewhere in my childhood I made a mental note that ended up etched on my heart: *Men hurt. Never live with one.*

So I never did. I picked men who wouldn't stay. Men who weren't available. Men who were married, engaged, dating others, lived out of state, or were addicted to alcohol or work. Men who would never completely commit. Nice guys who stuck around scared me until I finished years of therapy.

The counselor who healed my darkest, deepest wounds also gave me ground rules for dating. They were easy to remember. They spelled out the word *safe*. There were four things she wanted me to be mindful of and the first was most important:

Secret. Can the relationship pass public scrutiny? If a relationship has to be kept secret, you don't belong in it.

Abusive. Does it harm you or degrade you or your children in any way?

Feelings. Are you in the relationship to avoid painful feelings? Is it a mood-altering relationship?

Empty. Is it empty of caring and commitment?

It was a great starting point. From then on, I knew my

number one quality to look for in a man: availability. As soon as I was attracted to someone, I asked myself, Is he available for a relationship from the start? If not, there's nowhere to go.

Over time, I created my own list of dating tips:

Stay away from unavailable men. Men who aren't available include gay men, priests, geographically undesirable men, married men, men who are engaged to someone else, men who are afraid to tell others that they're dating you because it'll scare away other potential dates.

Keep no secrets. I have a dear friend whose husband cheated on her for years. It wasn't an affair, it was a lifestyle. Meanwhile, they were going through couples therapy, "working on the relationship." He pretended to participate in counseling sessions, never letting on about the other woman until the day he got caught and the marriage ended. Another friend kept bouncing back to a man who was married thinking he'd leave and marry her. I kept telling her, "If you marry a man who cheats on his wife, you marry a man who cheats on his wife." Same goes for men. If your girlfriend won't tell her sister, mother, friends, or her ex that she's dating you, move on. Don't be someone else's stash or side dish. If she can't be honest and open about dating you, dump her. Do you want an affair or a relationship?

Beware of addictions. If someone is hooked on drinking, gambling, pot, crack, lottery tickets, sex, work, et cetera, that person is not available. Beware of your own inner need to find and fix a broken soul. If you keep going for the fixer-upper, ask yourself why. If you think you can save him or her, think again. The first step in every 12-step program is to admit you are powerless.

Be the real deal. Be you 100 percent. One man I dated told me he liked everything about me except he thought I was too spiritual. Is there such a thing? What did he expect me to do, believe more in him and less in God? The thing I valued most in me he found hard to tolerate. I don't want someone who tolerates me. I want someone who celebrates me.

Tell the world what you want in a partner. Tell yourself first. Write it down. Get the shallow stuff out—the height, the weight, the income—release it, and let it go. Then sit in the quiet of your soul, go down to the core, and ask, What do I really want? Then make the list. At the bottom write: This or something better. Then tuck it away in a box and let it go.

Ignore the wrapper. The wrapping paper on a gift usually gives no indication of what is inside. Sometimes the wrap is better than the contents. Some of the best gifts come without a wrapper. Don't ignore the short bald guys or the chubby teddy-bear types. Before you write them off with the four-letter curse "nice," think long and hard about what you truly want. Don't overlook the softie with the tender heart for a tough guy with six-pack abs. The tender heart will outlive the washboard tummy. Ask any married woman over 40.

Create a greater you. Create and live a life that is so good, it doesn't matter if anyone comes along. Say yes to every opportunity to make new friends, meet new people, try new adventures. Get busy living the life of your dreams instead of looking for the man or woman of your dreams. It's like the proverbial butterfly: once you stop chasing it, it will gently land on your shoulder. Instead of looking for the right partner, become the right man or woman...for you. Be your best, deepest, truest self. Make yourself attractive to you.

There is somebody for everybody. If you're busy trying to turn yourself into someone else, Mr. Right might not be interested because he's looking for a woman like the one you just abandoned.

Everything Can Change in the Blink of an Eye. But Don't Worry; God Never Blinks.

In one of his novels, Chaim Potok describes how God sees versus how humans see. We see the world as fragmented, because we blink. But God, who never blinks, sees the entire universe as we cannot see it. Whole.

Imagine what we might see in a lifetime of not blinking?

Some people believe that a rare few others see in the blinks. The art critic Sister Maria Gloria Riva once told an interviewer that saints and artists can see between blinks. If you examine their creations, the beauty of wholeness shines through. They see with the vision of faith. To paraphrase her, if you have faith, you can see beyond the limitations of most vision. You can see the light of a "now" where others see only the darkness in the "not yet."

I once met a man who could see the now in the not yet. Everything in his life changed in the blink of an eye one Christmas.

Father Mike Surufka got the call while he was out of town on December 7, 2002. His home, the church rectory, was in flames. He rushed back to news that kept getting worse. His best friend, the church pastor, was missing. No one could find Father Willy.

Then the bishop called. Firefighters had found a body in the rubble. It was Father Willy. The investigation revealed a new horror. The priest didn't die in the fire. He had been shot. Who would murder Father William Gulas?

Everyone at St. Stanislaus Church in Cleveland's old Slavic Village loved Father Willy. He was pastor of the beautiful, ornate Polish church that the Franciscan priests shepherded. The day of the fire, Father Mike arrived at the church for five o'clock Mass just as the people prayed, "Lamb of God, have mercy on us." He held it together until he looked up and saw all the altar boys and girls. Every single one of them had showed up. They had called one another and come to the church. They stood there in cassocks, their faces soaked in tears.

Father Mike wept.

It got even tougher for him. Police charged a Franciscan brother for the murder. Brother Daniel Montgomery had lived with the two priests but had not yet taken final vows to be a Franciscan. His behavior was odd and made people uncomfortable. Father Willy had to break the news that it wasn't working out.

Brother Dan shot him. Then he set the rectory on fire to cover up the murder.

That night Father Mike lay in bed knowing he'd lost everything—his possessions, his home, his friend. He wandered through the rubble the next day, through blackened halls, the stink of smoke, the shards of glass, the bare wires.

He was homeless. His dear friend was gone. Everyone in the church was devastated. It was the most despair he'd ever felt. When he opened the door, a woman approached him. An angel, he calls her now.

"How are you?" she asked.

He told the truth. "I have nothing."

She looked at him and said three words that changed his life:

"You have us."

Since then, he's recalculated.

"I've got everything," he says.

That night took him to the essence of what it means to be Franciscan: when your only attachment is to God and to love, you have everything that matters. He had worn the long, simple brown robe of Saint Francis for 20 years, but that was the moment he became a Franciscan.

At the core of the Franciscan order is brotherhood. That's what made Father Willy's death even harder. A brother killed one of his own.

When Father Mike walked through the burned rectory, his sandals crunched shards of glass on the blackened carpet. He stopped in his old office, where pushpins were melted to the bulletin board, where photos of friends curled into black claws. He walked down the tunnel of black, past boarded-up windows, past charcoal doorframes, into a room that should be a chapel. On a wall blackened by smoke, a cross left its imprint in bright white — so bright, it seemed to glow in the dark.

He walked through the kitchen where he and Father Willy shared meals. He paused in the doorway where they found Father Willy. He stopped in the living room where they had

put up the Christmas tree. How would the people of the parish celebrate Christmas? How could they celebrate anything?

The people at St. Stanislaus knew that Christmas would be
tough, so they found the widest, tallest tree for the church. It
climbed 17 feet. They covered it in lights, and everyone from
this tough old Polish parish brought an ornament from home to
decorate it. It was the most glorious tree they had ever seen.

A smile comes over Father Mike whenever he talks about
that Christmas, the darkest and brightest Christmas of his life.
He picks up a worn black Bible bent nearly in half down the
middle, creased from being opened so often. He skims John
1:5 and grins when he finds the passage. "This is *so* Christmas,"
he says, then reads aloud:

*"The light shines on in darkness, a darkness that did not over-
come it."*

He closes the book. On the cover, on the bottom right corner, stamped in gold are two words: William Gulas.

It was Father Willy's Bible.

Saint Francis once said that there is no darkness that is so
dark that the light of a single candle cannot pierce it.

That woman was the candle.

A single flame.

A blink.

Life Is Too Short for Long Pity Parties. Get Busy Living, or Get Busy Dying.

My all-time favorite movie is *The Shawshank Redemption*.

If I had to sum up the movie in one word it would be this: hope.

The movie is based on a Stephen King short story. In the movie, actor Tim Robbins plays Andy, an innocent man serving a life sentence for killing his wife and her boyfriend. While in prison, the character endures beatings, gang rapes, and devastating despair. After years of abuse, something in Andy snaps, for the better. He sets his eyes on a lovely spot of beach in Mexico and decides he will get there. He doesn't tell a soul what he has planned, not even his best friend, Red, played by actor Morgan Freeman.

The scene that struck me most is when the two inmates are sitting in the prison yard. Andy tells Red that there's a place inside a person that no guard or warden can touch, a place no one can lock away.

Red warns him that it's dangerous to hope in a place like prison.

Andy refuses to believe him. He talks about going to the beach town to look at the stars, to touch the sand, to wade in the water and feel free.

Red is so disturbed by Andy's vision of freedom that he admonishes him not to dream at all. He warns him to remember his place, and points out that Mexico isn't it.

Andy seems to believe him when he whispers, "You're right. It's down there, and I'm in here."

He decides that it comes down to a simple choice: "Get busy living or get busy dying."

The next time we see Andy, he's in his cell clutching a rope. He's either going to take his life or set himself free.

Life constantly hands us those two choices: get busy living, or get busy dying. Which will you choose? How often do we choose correctly? What part of every day or any day do you simply feel free?

Someone once told me the difference between a rut and a grave is this: a rut has a little more room to move around. When I find myself in a rut, I know I better get out fast before it becomes a grave.

Let me tell you about one man who had every reason to stay stuck. Steve Barille was a senior running back and baseball catcher in high school back in 1976. One day, one average, ordinary day like any other, Steve tried out the trampoline in the Mayfield High School gym. He was 17 when he took his last step.

He jumped on the trampoline, then attempted a backflip. In the brief minutes between his landing and the arrival of the ambulance, he asked his gym teacher, "Can you live if you've broken your neck?"

He was paralyzed from the neck down. A quadriplegic. The neurosurgeon told Steve's mother, "I wouldn't wish this on my worst enemy." Steve was on a respirator for months. He was in hospitals for a year. But before he was even released, he started work on his psychology degree from John Carroll University.

Twenty years later, Steve uses a stick in his mouth to tap computer keys to call up his dissertation. The title made my eyes glaze over: "The Examiner Effect of a Physically Disabled Administrator When Using the Holtzman Ink Blot Technique to Assess Personality."

Steve wrote it without being able to turn a page, take a note, or even rub his tired eyes. He is now Dr. Barille, with a PhD in psychology from Kent State University. Steve calls his success a team victory. He gives credit to his family and friends. "It's about what is possible when you have the collective will. I had the installation of hope," he said. "When I thought it was too difficult, others didn't."

The bearded man zips through the hospital lobby in a chair that senses from the tilt of his head which way to turn and how fast to go. His hands lie frozen flat on small trays in front of him. He can't lift a finger to press an elevator button. He simply waits for someone to come along.

He watches his patients as they struggle to walk again in physical therapy. Some need help overcoming the fear of falling. Others need to be lifted out of depression at never being able to use one arm again. His gentle manner and soft voice comfort those who have suffered strokes, aneurysms, amputations, and spinal cord injuries.

His patients learn to move with the help of canes, braces, and walkers. To once again lift a fork, throw a ball, turn a steering wheel, all things Steve will never do. Yet he can't stop smiling. He calls it a privilege to help them emotionally adjust to a new life. He rejoices in every step they take, even though he'll never walk again.

"I really love what I'm doing. It's everything that people dream about," he told me. "It doesn't take much psychology to help them. The biggest thing is instilling hope."

From his wheelchair, he helps them overcome their fears. Fear of falling, fear of failing, fear of staying stuck in despair. They take one look at this free man in the wheelchair and know, it's time to get busy living.

You Can Get Through Anything Life Hands You if You Stay Put in the Day You Are in and Don't Jump Ahead.

There was a time in my life—years, actually—when strangers would stop me and ask if I was okay.

I walked with my head down, my coat wide open on a snowy, cold, windy day, no gloves, no hat, no scarf. I looked orphaned by life, like I didn't have a friend in the world, like I'd lost my best friend. People would stop to ask me, "Are you having a bad day?" I'd shake my head and tell them no. "I'm having a bad life." I meant it.

No one really has a bad life. Not even a bad day. Just bad moments.

Years of counseling and recovery meetings healed me, then years of spiritual retreats transformed me, closing up the hole in me so the love flowing in from family and friends no longer leaked out. Then along came the man of my dreams. More love than my heart could hold overflowed and spilled out onto others.

I basked in a nearly constant awareness that life is good. It took decades of hard work, but I was at a new place. I loved life and life loved me. I created a vision board of the future of my dreams. Teaching. Retreats. Books. A syndicated column. Giving away all the gifts life had given me.

Then along came cancer.

Needless to say, it wasn't on my vision board. Breast cancer plunged me into a long, drawn-out suffering that exceeded nearly anything in my past. Each day I had a choice: dwell on the misery of cancer treatments or look for the joy in simply being alive.

It wasn't easy.

It was like a living Where's Waldo? book. Instead of looking for the weird guy in the striped hat, I was trying to figure out where to find something good in a day in which food tasted like metal, meals didn't stay down, strangers stared at my bald head, and the woman standing at the mirror didn't recognize her own reflection.

The treatment wasn't as bad as my attitude toward it. I suffered because I wasn't living in the present moment. I was dwelling on yesterday, counting up all the days that I felt sick. Then I spent time dreading the future, the next chemotherapy appointment, the side effects it would bring, the meals I'd throw up, the fatigue that radiation would invite once the chemo was over.

The only way through it all was to stop dwelling on what yesterday brought (good or bad) and what tomorrow might bring (good or bad). The only day worth living was the one I was in. Those 24 hours were do-able as long as I didn't drag the past and future into them. One day of cancer was bearable if that's all I had to get through.

It took constant discipline to ignore the calendar. It took vigilance to put blinders on to block out every day except the one called today. I made every day a do-over. Each morning, I would start from scratch: forget all about yesterday, and not even think about tomorrow. I'd try to just live in today.

I took the advice of an old woman I met on a retreat. Every morning, rain or shine, snow or sleet, she would open her bedroom window, take a deep breath, and greet the day with these words: "This is the day that the Lord has made. I will rejoice in it and be glad."

This.

This is the day. Not yesterday. Not tomorrow. This day.

I didn't open the window, but I started every morning with those words and still do. Some days I add, "Thank you, God, for another day of life. Give me the grace to live this day deeply, fully, and joyfully."

Once I blocked out everything except the present moment, joy seeped into my life. Not hours and hours of glee, but tender, sweet moments that I no longer missed because my head was galloping off into tomorrow or wallowing around in yesterday.

Even with treatments long behind me, there are days when fear grips me by the throat and almost steals my day by whispering, "What if the cancer returns? What if you can't write anymore? What if you lose everything you love?"

Some days, 24 hours is too much to stay put in, so I take

the day hour by hour, moment by moment. I break the task, the challenge, the fear into small, bite-size pieces. I can handle a *piece* of fear, depression, anger, pain, sadness, loneliness, illness. I actually put my hands up to my face, one next to each eye, like blinders on a horse. It's my way to remember to stay put in now. Blinders make horses stay focused on what is in front of them. With blinders, they can't see to the side and get scared or distracted. They can't see what is going to happen, so they keep putting one hoof in front of the other and keep moving. I put my blinders on and tell myself, no looking at tomorrow, no looking at yesterday, then take a step and another and another.

Andre Dubus once wrote in "A Father's Story": "It is not hard to live through a day, if you can live through a moment. What creates despair is the imagination, which pretends there is a future, and insists on predicting millions of moments, thousands of days, and so drains you that you cannot live the moment at hand."

I no longer squander today being afraid of tomorrow or wallowing in guilt or resentments of the past. God isn't present in the past or future. The great I Am is in the present moment. When I claim that presence, I can get through anything today.

That's all that is required of any of us, to live today.

A Writer Is Someone Who Writes. If You Want to Be a Writer, Write.

Wₑ snaked outside for a block, shivering in the wind.

Writers and wannabe writers lined up outside the chapel at Case Western Reserve University. It looked like a convention of clones. Nearly everyone who showed up for "A Conversation with Anne Lamott" was female and middle-aged and wore the same hungry look in their eyes.

We all came to meet the woman on our nightstand. She showed up with dreadlocks tied up in a twisted scarf on her head, glasses, faded blue jeans, and a long-sleeved white shirt that looked about as elegant as long underwear, but on her, it worked. Lamott tries to cooperate with grace by taking three small steps: slow down, breathe, take a walk. Hers is a holiness full of holes.

She once wrote, "When God is going to do something wonderful, He or She always starts with a hardship; when God is going to do something amazing, He or She starts with an impossibility."

I first discovered her by reading *Bird by Bird: Some Instructions on Writing and Life*. Most writers have read it. It's become a classic. The title came from the day her brother, who was ten at the time, was struggling to write a report on birds. He had three months to finish it but waited until the last minute to start. He sat at the table, nearly in tears, surrounded by books on birds he hadn't opened. His dad comforted him with these words: "Bird by bird, buddy. Just take it bird by bird."

Writing is that simple. So are most seemingly overwhelming projects and plans we undertake if we take them piece by piece, bird by bird.

Finish one short story. One poem. Make a commitment to finishing things. And if you don't know where to start, start with your childhood.

She told us to write what wants to be written. Ask yourself: How alive are you willing to be? Quiet the voices in your head, whether they be from parents, teachers, or the culture around you. Then sit down and write a crappy first draft.

She talked about listening to the nudge of the Holy Spirit, that inner voice, that intuitive hunch. The most ordinary people listen to that creative call, she said. Just tell your stories and tell them in your own voice. That's all people are looking for, she said.

Can it be that easy? Where do you find stories to tell?

"They are in you, like jewels in your heart," she said.

We left without any clue about how to get published. But we all knew where to begin: Word by word. Line by line. Bird by bird.

It's a starting place most people avoid. People are always asking me how to be a writer. I don't know, but here's how not to be one.

Watch hours of mindless TV. Check your e-mail. Instant message your friends. Visit a chat room of writers. Answer the phone every time it rings.

Fret over whether it's who or whom, lie or lay, its or it's, you and I or you and me.

Agonize over whether to use colons or semicolons.

Spend hours pondering over using longhand or shorthand, computer or legal pad, pen or pencil, blue ink or black, Macintosh or PC.

Recall every bad writing grade you ever got. Replay scenes in your head of every teacher who ever criticized your work. Hold debates with the invisible editors who call a meeting in your head every hour. Weep over rejection letters you haven't yet received but are sure you will.

How not to write?

Let technology scare you. Postpone writing until you learn how to electronically number all the pages.

Get your doctorate in creative writing first. Start therapy. Find the right writers' group.

Wait until you get over your fear of rejection or fear of success. Tell yourself the odds of getting published are against you. Worry about how you'll pay the bills. Compare yourself to everyone else.

Complain that it's too hot, too cold, too muggy, or too nice outside to write.

Try hard to add significantly to the world of great literature.

Analyze every idea before you write the first sentence. Strive for perfection. Declare yourself the next Shakespeare.

Try to write like anyone except yourself. Use only big words to impress people.

How not to write? Sign up for another writers' conference instead of actually writing.

Constantly tell yourself you have nothing to say. Consult your horoscope. Make a list of all the people who don't think you'll cut it as a writer.

File your nails. Water the plants. Clean the basement.

Open an office. Build a hermitage in the backyard or an entire wing on the house to write in.

Look for affirmation from everyone around you. Ignore your own sorrows, passions, and music. Whine about how nobody understands you.

Demand an advance first.

Talk to telemarketers. Play solitaire on the computer. Make a to-do list with writing as the top priority.

Complain about the English teacher who scarred you. The professor who ignored you. The brother who stole your diaries. The sister who read your journals.

Waste time envying other writers who have it so easy.

Edit as you go. Check the rules of grammar and punctuation before you finish every paragraph.

Talk about your ideas so much that even you lose interest.

How not to write? Wait until you have children. Wait until your children stop teething, finish soccer season, and go off to college. Wait until you have two hours of uninterrupted time to write.

Wait until you quit smoking, quit drinking, or find the right drink and are stone drunk.

Wait until your siblings move and your parents die. Wait until you meet the love of your life. Wait until the divorce is final.

Wait until you go on vacation. Wait until vacation is over. Wait until you retire.

Wait until you find your muse. Wait until you feel inspired.

Wait until a doctor says you've got six months to live.

Then die with your words still inside of you.

19

It's Never Too Late to Have a Happy Childhood. But the Second One Is Up to You and No One Else.

For the first 30 years of my life, I hated my birthday.

It always reminded me of the big mistake that I was, or felt that I was. No matter what present I got, it didn't touch that place inside of me that felt so forgotten and alone.

The comedian George Carlin, when asked how old he was, once replied, "I'm one, I'm two, I'm three, I'm four, I'm five..." and on and on up until his present age.

It's true. Somewhere inside us we are all the ages we have ever been. We're the 3-year-old who got bit by the dog. We're the 6-year-old our mother lost track of at the mall. We're the 10-year-old who got tickled till we wet our pants. We're the 13-year-old shy kid with zits. We're the 16-year-old no one asked to the prom, and so on. We walk around in the bodies of adults until someone presses the right button and summons up one of those kids.

Some people had unhappy childhoods. Others had unhappy moments. How do you heal a childhood?

You give yourself a new, happy one. You feed the child or children that you still carry inside of you.

One year I went out and bought myself a pair of baby shoes. My mom had 11 kids. We didn't get a baby book to save. She didn't bronze our first pair of shoes. She didn't save anything from our infanthood because it got passed down to the next child or had already been a hand-me-down.

The first four children born filled the photo album. They're in professional photographs, grinning in the perfect soft light. I was number five. There are no baby pictures. Or maybe there are. Those random shots of that child in a playpen, in a crib, in a stroller could be me. Or is it Mary? Or Tom? No one can tell. It used to make me sad that my mom saved no mementos of original, unique me as a baby and toddler. That's probably why I saved everything my daughter owned. Her first sneakers. Her first blue jeans. Her first bra.

Then one day, I decided to stop feeling sorry for myself and create my own mementos. I bought a newborn's size pair of silky white slippers with pearly buttons. They were the dainty shoes I wished my mom had bought and saved for me. I even picked out a pretty rattle and claimed it as mine.

As silly or strange as it sounds, it helped close the wound a little and build some scar tissue over a place that kept opening, a place I kept falling into.

My parents gave me the best childhood they could. One better than both of them had combined. Now that I'm an adult, it's no longer up to them to make my childhood better. That job is all mine.

It's up to me to look back at my childhood and find the joy that was. To look into my life and see the joy that is. To look into my future and build the joy that can be.

It's up to me to make magic. Same goes for you. Arrange a playdate with yourself. Schedule in or stumble upon one hour of pure fun each week. Take your inner child—or children—on a weekly outing. I suggested it at a women's retreat and got dozens of ideas to pass on:

Take yourself to a toy store and spend $10 on fun.

Go to the closest planetarium and wish on some stars.

Make a volcano with baking soda and vinegar.

Eat an Eskimo Pie, a Drumstick, or a fudgesicle for breakfast.

Play 18 holes of miniature golf.

Make s'mores.

Eat dessert first.

Fingerpaint an old bedsheet.

Watch cartoons in your pajamas.

Rent a Three Stooges video.

Make cinnamon toast for breakfast.

Eat Cheerios before bed.

Play Ping-Pong.

Pick a bouquet of dandelions.

Read the funny pages out loud with dramatic voices for each part.

Read with a flashlight under the covers.

Go to the pet store and hug kittens.

Visit the kids' section of a bookstore.

Play on swings.

Run through a cornfield.

Pretend you're invisible all day.

Play a game without keeping score.

Go on a scavenger hunt.

Buy a 64-pack of Crayolas and don't share them with anybody.

Perform somersaults in the front yard.

Have a grass fight with the lawn clippings.

Walk in the rain without an umbrella.

Ride your bike through mud puddles.

Play Candyland, Go Fish, or Chutes and Ladders.

Go hunting for bird's nests.

Read *Winnie the Pooh*, then go hunting for woozles.

Play badminton in the front yard.

Make Boston coolers (root beer floats to some folks).

Have a picnic on the floor during the winter.

Make a banana split.

Dress up fancy and play croquet in the yard.

Watch *Mary Poppins*.

Play hooky from work.

Do nothing all day.

Watch clouds, ants, squirrels, and leaves move.

Create a wild hairdo out of wet shampooed hair.

Memorize "Bear in There" ("There's a polar bear in our Frigidaire") from *A Light in the Attic* by Shel Silverstein.

Toast marshmallows on the kitchen stove.

Play the license plate game.

Build a fort with sheets and tables.

Color with crayons between your toes.

Make necklaces of seashells or buckeyes.

Make music by clinking on water-filled glasses.

Visit the fire station to see the trucks.

Camp in the backyard or on the porch or on the living room floor.

Hold a cartwheel contest with the neighbors.

Draw with sidewalk chalk.

Skip stones across a river, look under rocks for critters, go wading in a creek.

Run through sprinklers in the summer, make snow angels in the winter.

Find a tire swing and hog it for an hour.

Host a pillow fight.

Go to an animal shelter and walk a dog.

Follow animal tracks wherever they go.

Have a fashion show with all your clothes.

Catch fireflies.

Visit the monkeys at the zoo.

Take yourself to a candy counter and spend $3.

Walk around holding a mirror so when you look in it it's like you're walking on the ceiling.

Climb a tree and read a comic book.

Practice cheerleading in the front yard.

Fly a kite.

Take ten quarters and try out every gumball machine at the supermarket.

Jump on the bed until you grow too tired and fall asleep.

Whatever you do, it's up to you.

It's never too late to have a happy childhood. Go for it. This one is up to you.

When It Comes to Going After What You Love in Life, Don't Take No for an Answer.

Ever since I read *Harriet the Spy* in the fifth grade I wanted to be a writer.

I filled journals and diaries but was too afraid to let anyone see what was in them. I spied on my brothers and sisters, poked around in their dresser drawers, and took notes on what I found, including pictures of my brother's friends mooning the camera. But when I got older and had the chance to actually work on the high school newspaper and do real writing, I was too afraid to.

In college, I changed my major from biology to botany to conservation and planned to be a forest ranger. Then I got pregnant and dropped out of school. When I returned six years later, it was time to pursue the dream.

At Kent State University I took a creative writing class. The first day, the professor had us each write on an index card why we were taking the class. I assumed the card was for his eyes only. I gushed about how much I loved to write. It read like a diary entry. He collected the cards, shuffled them, pulled one card out, and sent us all to the board. He told us to write down the sentences that he read. All four walls held chalkboards. Classmates wrote my feeble sentences over them all. I turned red as a fire truck.

The entire class studied my rambling paragraph, then tore it to shreds, analyzing the grammar, structure, tone, and content. I prayed for the power to evaporate. I never could get back on track in that class. I felt like a failure from day one.

The next semester I switched from English to public relations and took my first journalism class. The first week I turned an assignment in late. The professor shamed me in front of the class. "Brett, you might as well drop out now because you're never going to make it."

I showed him. He wanted us to turn in 8 inches of copy a week, about 250 words. I turned in double the amount. No way was I flunking this class. I got an A, but even better, an arm-twisting. Two professors stopped me in the hall and told me to major in journalism. They found me an $800 scholarship to help cover books and supplies. Journalism was the perfect fit.

When it was time to graduate, I desperately needed a job in the field. I was working as an alcoholism counselor part time, earning $7,000 a year. I sent out 30 résumés to newspapers all over the country. I got 30 rejection letters. Desperate, I put together a package of the best work I'd written for the college newspaper. I approached my law of mass communications professor at Kent State for a job. He worked at the *Beacon*

Journal, the best paper in the area, a Knight-Ridder paper, one of the best chains in the business.

The professor barely glanced at my work. He shook his head and said I wasn't ready for a paper that good, that it would be years until I was, if ever. It felt like a door slamming in my face. I trembled and held back the tears until I got to my car, then cried the whole way home.

But I couldn't afford to take no for an answer. I had a child to feed and I wanted to feed her something more than peanut butter and jelly sandwiches and mac and cheese. I wanted a career, not just a job. I ended up taking a job at the only newspaper that would have me. The Lorain *Journal* hired me to cover city hall. It wasn't the beat I wanted or the city or the paycheck, but it was a job in the field of my dreams. I said yes to every assignment, even the ones I hated. I made time to write extra stories and sent my best articles to my friend Bill who worked at the *Beacon Journal* to get feedback to make them better.

Six months later, an editor at the *Beacon Journal* called and offered me a job. Bill had passed along my writing. I took the job, even though it was writing for the business section about health insurance and farming, which I knew nothing about. I did that for a while, then covered social services and breaking news and wrote magazine stories. After a few years, I decided I wanted to write a column. I wanted to tell my own personal truth, not just be an objective bystander reporting news stories.

The editor of the paper told me no, he didn't need or want another columnist. I cried my eyes out in the restroom, then went home and brainstormed what would make my column different. I jotted down a few ideas and met with the editor again. He said no but couched it with a puppy pat on the head and told me I was too good a reporter to lose to a column.

I refused to let his no sink in. I used it as fuel. I wrote a long list of column ideas. I typed out six sample columns, including my introductory column. It was a bold move, but I had to do it. I was prepared and psyched when I presented it all to him. He still said no. I cried all the way home. My husband (boyfriend at the time), Bruce, held my hand, wiped my tears, then said, Okay, now what's the next step to getting what you want?

The next step? Bruce wouldn't take no for an answer. He's a chronic optimist. There's an old story about a set of twin boys. One was a born optimist, the other, a born pessimist. A psychiatrist trying to understand them put the pessimist in a room full of toys to see what would happen. The boy whined and cried. The doctor put the optimist in a room full of horse manure and gave the boy a shovel. Hours later, the optimist was still grinning and shoveling the manure as fast as he could. Why was he so happy? The boy said, "With all this manure, there's got to be a pony in here somewhere!"

That's Bruce. No matter how bad a situation looks, he starts looking for the pony. He wouldn't let me surrender my dreams to someone else's no. There's no such thing as no, he said. Find a way to make it a yes.

I decided then and there: I am a columnist. I am a columnist who just doesn't happen to have a column yet. So I shoveled away, looking for columns. I wrote first-person stories every chance I got. On Twins Day, an assignment most reporters dread, I wrote about what it was like to be at the event all alone, minus a double. On National Vegetarian Day, I wrote a column about what it was like to celebrate Thanksgiving with nut loaf instead of turkey.

In time, I wore the editor down. He said yes. I've been writing columns ever since 1994 when he finally opened the door I'd been pushing on.

Every day I pinch myself.

I have a dream job. All because I wouldn't take no for an answer and kept shoveling.

Burn the Candles, Use the Nice Sheets, Wear the Fancy Lingerie. Don't Save Anything for a Special Occasion. Today Is Special Enough.

I no longer dust my candles.

I used to be guilty of that. Friends gave me lovely scented candles, cinnamon apple, French vanilla, harvest spice, or aromatherapy peace, love, and harmony candles with leaves and rose petals pressed into the sides. The candles all went unlit.

I didn't want to use them up, so I dusted them. Month after month, year after year. Someone once bought me a candle set into a glass globe surrounded by baby's breath. I had it for years until one day I went to dust it and the wax had melted in the hot sun.

I knew better than to ignore my candles. I had grown up reading my mother's favorite columnist, Erma Bombeck. Erma was the first newspaper columnist I ever read. She was a humorist and a housewife and the only writer who made my mother laugh out loud. My mom had every Erma book. After

Erma got breast cancer, her writing got even more poignant. Two years later, her kidneys failed from a genetic disorder. She died after getting a transplant.

In one of her best columns, she reflected on what she would have done differently in life if she had the chance to do it all over again. Every time I finished reading it, I vowed to honor it.

I resolved to quit checking e-mail while talking to my mom on the phone, to stop multitasking and be more present, to hang up my cell phone and enjoy the view from my windshield.

I promised to spend more time outdoors and not fret about my hair frizzing in the rain or my bangs going flat from the humidity.

I planned to light more fires in the fireplace and not worry about how cold it would make the house later or how smoky it would make the living room.

I decided to be more spontaneous with my friends and join them for last-minute dinners, to talk less about my world and listen more about what was going on in theirs.

But I always failed to keep those promises to change. Until I got cancer.

When I was 41, I found a lump the size of a grape in my right breast. Stage II, fast-growing cancer. I ended up bald, sick, and exhausted from two surgeries, four rounds of chemo, and six weeks of daily radiation treatments. Ah, but I got to live. I got to live a brand-spanking-new life.

Cancer is a great wake-up call. A call to take the tag off the new lingerie and wear that black lacy slip. To open the box of pearls and put them on. To use the fireplace. To crack open the bath oil beads before they shrivel up in a bowl on the toilet tank. To light the candles.

I carry a picture of me bald in my wallet to remind me that every day aboveground is a good day. That, and I see a reminder on my heart every day where there is no breast. My scars remind me that we all have an expiration date, a shelf life. It isn't stamped on us like it is on a carton of milk or a tub of cottage cheese, but we're all terminal. Nobody lives forever.

Cancer taught me to stop saving things for a special occasion, because every day is special. Use it all, spend it all now. I'm not referring to money, but to the advice of writer Annie Dillard.

Her wisdom in *The Writing Life* applies to writing but also to living.

She advises writers to use all their material now. Don't save an anecdote, paragraph, quote, beginning or ending for some better novel or poem or short story you plan to write sometime in the future. The fact that you want to use it means you should.

It takes an act of faith. You have to trust that once you use up the good stuff, more good stuff will appear. The well will fill back up.

I have stacks and stacks of journals and diaries in my bookshelf waiting for the right moment, the right project, the right book. Waiting. How long will I wait? How long will you?

Frank McCourt was 66 when *Angela's Ashes* was published. Laura Ingalls Wilder published her first book at 65. Folk artist Grandma Moses kicked off her painting career in her 70s.

It moved me to read that Michelangelo scrawled this note as both a warning and an invitation to his young apprentice

Antonio: "Draw, Antonio, draw, Antonio, draw and do not waste time."

I imagined placing a note on my mirror that read, *Live, Regina, live, Regina, live and do not waste time.*

You don't have to get cancer to start living life to the fullest. Life is too short to waste doing anything boring or joyless. My post-cancer philosophy? No wasted time. No ugly clothes. No boring movies. Cancel them all. Put joy and beauty in their place.

Cancer taught me two important words and when to use them. I can now say the word *no*. When friends ask me to go to an event and I don't want to, I say, "No, and thank you for asking." No more saying yes to what I don't want to do. I ask myself, Is this worth trading hours of my life?

I used to say yes when I wanted to say no, usually out of fear of what people would think of me if I said no. Saying no means I can say yes. Yes to an authentic life I truly enjoy living. Yes to being with the people I love most so I'll never regret that I didn't stay in touch. Yes to lighting the candles, wearing the pearls, using the good china, walking in the rain, or making angels in the snow even though I might track mud or slush in the house.

These three simple steps can change your life:

1. Choose one thing you need to say no to.

It could be an unhealthy relationship...with a man, a credit card, a donut shop. You know what it is. Choose that one thing. What would happen if you started saying no? No to projects that don't need to be done by you. No to every person at church or school or work who asks you to donate your time and talent to one more committee or commitment. Take a look at your calendar. Is there anything on there this month that you really want to do? Grab some sticky notes and mark out places for you, for joy, passion, and love.

2. Choose one thing you need and want to say yes to.

It could be loving yourself as is, waistline and all. Forgiving someone you miss. Going back to school, retiring early, trying to date again. You know deep inside what it is. When you say no, you can start saying yes. Yes to slower days, weekend hikes, reading great books, oil painting, a trip to Hawaii, piano lessons, pedicures. Say yes to what enhances your life and the world around you. We're not talking a big leap. Just the next small step. What is yours?

3. Share those two things — that yes and that no — with your biggest cheerleader. Tell your spouse, your friend, your parent. Make it real.

You don't need a cancer verdict to start living more fully. Every day, light a candle. What a great reminder that life is short, that the only time that matters is now. Walk out of boring movies. Close any book that doesn't dazzle you.

Greet every morning with open arms and say thanks every night with a full heart. Each day is a precious gift to be savored and used, not left unopened and hoarded for a future that may never come.

Overprepare, Then Go with the Flow.

Most everything in life still scares me.

I used to think if I prayed the right way or prayed the right prayers, all the fear would leave me. And it does leave. Only problem is, it comes rushing back the next time I face a new challenge. There's an old saying, "Courage is fear that has said its prayers." I pray constantly. My prayers don't always make the fear go away. The prayers give me the grace to take action anyway, to walk or run through the fear, depending upon the challenge.

Fear is my constant, annoying life companion. My new answer to fear is this: So what? Bring on the next challenge.

My friend Don taught me a motto that has gotten him through job interviews, grant writing, and high-level executive meetings that terrified him at the time. It's gotten me through giving commencement addresses to hundreds, writing columns on deadline for hundreds of thousands of readers, and hosting a live weekly radio show. It even helped me coach a friend through childbirth.

Don first learned of the slogan when he was an addiction specialist staffing a state teenage program in the 1980s. He was given tons of information to share with the 12 children he had to shepherd during weeklong support groups. In the training sessions, the head trainer always said, "Overprepare and go with the flow." Great advice when you're working with teenagers. Don used that motto, and his sessions with the kids allowed for lots of personal sharing because he went with the flow, even though he had enough information to fall back on in case the flow came to an abrupt stop. His kids loved the discussions so much, they nicknamed their group Daddy D and the Dirty Dozen and didn't want them to end.

Over the years, Don used the phrase to guide him anytime he had to present information he felt uncertain about. When he applied for jobs, he wrote a business plan that included all the information he could obtain about the organization. He identified things that needed to be done and explained how he would do it. For one job, he interviewed 25 professionals in the field and put together two notebooks of information. Of course he got hired.

Now he approaches every unfamiliar situation by putting in extra time and preparing more than anyone else. He used to be envious of guys he thought were smarter than him. Then he realized the only difference between him and them was that they did their homework. They overprepared. He started doing the same and let the flow carry him along, past them.

I've used his motto every week to prepare for the radio

show I host weekly on NPR's Cleveland affiliate. Every week the topic and guests change but that open microphone stays the same. I used to feel anxiety rising as soon as I woke up the morning of the show. Not anymore. I overprepare the day before, print out pages of background, research the guests and topics. I spread the information out before me and just seeing it gives me confidence. I hardly ever use half of it. But as soon as I'm behind the microphone and we go live, the anxiety is gone and I have a ball.

When my friend Sharon asked me to be her birthing coach, I was excited but scared. I'd had a baby but had never coached anyone through childbirth.

We attended classes together for weeks. I took copious notes. I transferred them onto giant index cards, categorized them, and color-coded them for the various stages of labor so we could use them quickly, like flash cards. I typed up a four-page birth plan that included the way she wanted to give birth: naturally, with the lights dim, no pain medicine or IVs, and soft music playing. I listed the visitors allowed and what scent of lotion to pack (rose) and what flavor of Gatorade to have on hand (Blue Frost).

When it came close to her delivery date, I packed a giant suitcase on wheels and filled it with everything the trainer suggested might be useful during childbirth: A CD player for soft music. A fountain to help her relax. A giant ball to sit on during labor. Posters of affirmations to cheer her on. Granola bars for me. Candy for the nurses. A video camera, stopwatch, and cigars. I made sure the baby seat was installed in the car, the gas tank was full, and the passenger seat was protected by a waterproof sheet.

We were ready for anything. My friend's water broke at 5 a.m. Talk about going with the flow. We arrived at the hospital and she got prepped in labor and delivery. For hours, nothing happened. I was prepared for that. We read magazines and books, played cards, and listened to music. Since she wasn't making enough progress, the medical team decided to induce labor, which wasn't in the plan. They put her on an IV drip. Once contractions started, they never stopped. I pulled out the index cards and helped her try different poses and breathing exercises to ease the discomfort and stay focused. In her worst pain, when she was struggling to get through endless contractions, I stayed calm and steady as a rock. When it was time to push, she pushed so hard her IV popped out. So did the baby.

Little Finnegan was gorgeous. His birth taught me that you can do anything, and more importantly, you can help others do anything. You just have to believe you can. And if you really prepare, it's a lot easier to trust the flow of life and where it will take you.

Be Eccentric Now. Don't Wait for Old Age to Wear Purple.

Old people and children know how to live.

The folks who are the bookends of life have the most fun. They don't care what anyone thinks. They're either too young to know better or too old to care.

Those of us in the middle could learn a thing or two from them.

Back in the 1980s, a poem about being bold enough to wear purple became wildly popular. Many people mistakenly call it "The Purple Poem," "Old Woman," or "When I'm Old I'll Wear Purple." The English poet Jenny Joseph wrote "Warning" in 1961. The poem ended up on greeting cards, sweatshirts, and handbags.

Like so many of us, the poet is tired of sensible shoes that match outfits we don't even like, clothes that make you blend in like wallpaper, acting so proper that no one notices you're alive because you don't jaywalk, don't utter a damn or a dang, don't make anyone blush, laugh, or sing. She's tired of behaving. Me, too.

Sometimes you just want to stand in a crowded elevator facing the wrong way and quote Shakespeare's *Hamlet* or sing "Zip-A-Dee-Doo-Dah" to the passengers. Some days you wish you had a kazoo in a board meeting or could break into a tap dance while standing in line at the post office. How fun life would be if more people adopted the eccentric's motto, "If you're going to go—go all out," or at least wore more purple.

Anytime I see a woman "of a certain age" wearing purple, I think of that poem. How boring to be so sensible all the time, to be a good example, to follow all the rules. I love the birthday card that reads, "If you follow all the rules, you miss all of the fun!"

"Warning" inspired a group of women to create the Red Hat Society. Women 50 and over gather to have fun and act silly. The "dis-organization," as it likes to call itself, has few rules. The women wear full regalia: a red hat, the more outlandish the better, and purple attire. Women under 50 are urged to wear a pink hat and lavender clothes. They haven't yet earned the right to be as flamboyant as their elders.

I secretly admire those women you see wearing red sequined blouses out to dinner on a Monday night or men donning giant Cat in the Hat Dr. Seuss hats to go to ball games. Most days I'm not even daring enough to wear lipstick. The first time I did, a woman at work asked me if I was sick. Guess I went a shade too purple.

The most eccentric thing I've done so far in my life is carry a Charlie Brown lunch box to school ... at college. It even had a cute little thermos with Lucy and Woodstock for my juice.

I never owned a lunch pail until I was 19. As a kid, I lived two blocks away from the grade school, so I walked home for lunch. The problem with carrying a lunch pail in your freshman year of college is that people won't talk to you. They assumed I had arrived on the short bus. My lunch pail embarrassed my friends, so I succumbed to normalcy.

A decade later, I tried wearing a black beret perched on the side of my head, but people teased me about being an artist or spoke French to me.

Why be normal? It's easier. But it isn't as much fun. Most of us are pretty normal. I looked up the word *eccentric* on Wikipedia once, and under the alphabetical listing found only six letters of examples. What a shame.

The categories listed were:

A. Acted as own attorney. B. Bow tie wearers and bird-watchers. D. Drag queens. P. Policy debaters. R. Rail transport modelers. W. Whistleblowers.

Not very eccentric at all, if you ask me. What about all those obvious categories?

C for cat lovers who have 26 or more felines hanging from chandeliers, bedposts, and curtains.

E for Einstein hairstyles that look like you just stuck your finger in a socket.

G for gnome lovers whose front yards give neighbors the creeps.

H for hoarders who collect Looney Tunes Pez containers.

M for monocle wearers who want to look menacing.

P for piercings that extend beyond ears to private parts.

S for Shriners who dress funny and ride those goofy cars during parades.

U for unicycle riders.

I've not met too many true eccentrics. I knew an old woman who wore only white from head to toe. Every so often I run into a man who wears shorts all year long. In Cleveland. Short ones, the kind that went out in the '80s. It's a little scary when he sits down. You have to avert your eyes or get flashed.

We do have one eccentric neighbor. Mr. H has worn the same clothes for ten years. They've disintegrated on him. His white T-shirt turned newspaper yellow; his blue work pants have holes in the knees bigger than the waistband. He's 80 and lives off a fortune he inherited.

Mr. H owns three houses on our street but lives in only one. The other two? He let them decay. Raccoons and squirrels moved in. Fine with him. He looks and acts like the Lorax. Trim a tree branch and he'll hit you with a rake. He's been arrested for not mowing his lawn. He wants to provide refuge for bunnies and such.

One day he came over with a bottle of burgundy nail polish and a receipt for 69 cents. He rang our doorbell and pointed out that a fleck of paint the size of a newborn's fingernail had fallen off the trim on our house. He wanted us to patch it up. Oh, and he wanted to be reimbursed for the 69 cents. He wouldn't take a dollar. Just the 69 cents, please.

Guys like him give the world texture.

Usually you hear about them when they die. The man who attended classes in Berkeley, California (where else?), in the nude. The man who named himself Joybubbles and could whistle out numbers to sound like a phone dialing. The woman whose obituary mentioned that she broke her leg at 80 when she fell out of a tree.

Once during a retreat at the Abbey of Gethsemani in Kentucky, I noticed one of the monks wasn't wearing shoes or sandals. When his white robe swished as he walked, it revealed cowboy boots. How cool.

If a monk can wear cowboy boots, the rest of us can accessorize better.

I've taken to wearing a pair of Cheetah sunglasses. I found them in South Beach, Florida, when my father-in-law died. We were at a sunglass store on Lincoln Road and I put them on as a joke. Who would ever wear something so wicked and wild?

My husband and his brother Gary loved them. My father-in-law loved sunglasses, so we all picked out a pair. I wore the Cheetah sunglasses to the funeral. Years later, I wore them to my daughter's wedding. They've become my signature.

I love author Ray Bradbury's quote about all of us being miracles of the Life Force. He makes you feel like you're a living, breathing exclamation point created by a universe that simply wants to shout itself and everyone in it alive.

I think that's what being eccentric is all about, being one of the shouts of the universe. So what are you waiting for?

Go shout!

Start Saving 10 Percent for Retirement as Soon as You Get Your First Paycheck.

For the first time in my life, I was making big money.

Okay, it wasn't big money, but it was a decent salary. For someone else, $22,000 a year was probably an indecent salary, but being the sole provider for a child on a salary of $7,500 a year for two years in a row, then getting a whopping $12,000 a year, hitting $22,000 a year seemed like a windfall.

I could take my daughter to McDonald's and not have to dig for quarters under the couch cushions. I could buy a pint of ice cream without waiting for it to go on sale. I could pay every utility bill on time.

Yes, I'd hit the big time. Or so I thought. I was in my thirties and still catching up to everyone else when the guy across from me at work started pestering me about saving for retirement. Retirement? He was nuts. I needed that money now. Retirement was decades away. Light-years.

I finally got a solid income and he wanted me to squander it on the future? That's how I saw it. Every couple of months, he'd start up and ask me if I was contributing in the company's 401(k) plan. The newspaper I worked for, the *Beacon Journal*, was owned by Knight-Ridder. The company put in a quarter for every dollar I put in. On a bigger scale, that meant for every $20, they put in $5. For every hundred, they put in $25, and so on.

No, I wasn't signed up for it and didn't plan on it. It wasn't simply that I didn't trust others with my money. I didn't trust money. I misunderstood that Bible quote, "The love of money is the root of all evil." I thought money was evil. Wasn't it greed to want more? A 401(k) sounded like a scheme to me. So I continued to turn down free money, not just the 25 percent match, but all that compounding interest.

My friend finally wore me down. "They're *giving* you money. How can you turn it down?" I finally contributed to that 401(k), but lost years of earning potential because of my fear and ignorance.

It wasn't until I met my husband years later that I learned the power of compounding. He introduced me to one of the most important financial concepts: compound interest. Albert Einstein is alleged to have said, "The most powerful force in the universe is compound interest."

If only I'd known all those years earlier that time makes money grow. I once had a CD with a few hundred dollars. Every two years when it opened up, I took out the interest and spent it. It was my bonus. Free money. Woo-hoo! I never let interest build. No one taught me to let interest grow on the interest I already earned. That way the money does the work for you. You can invest it in stocks, mutual funds, that's between you and a financial adviser. Just leave it alone—all of it—even the interest. You can have the money taken out of your paycheck through direct deposit. You learn to live on what is left.

One of the simplest and most popular books that explains it is *The Wealthy Barber*, by David Chilton. It was written in 1989 and contains an eternal truth. The premise is that Roy, a small-town wealthy barber, serves as a mentor to his patrons. He tells them to start contributing right away to retirement, no matter how old they are. The earlier the better. In fact, the earlier, the best.

Roy tells the story of 22-year-old twins who decided to start saving for retirement. One twin opens an IRA, invests $2,000 a year for six years, and then stops. The story works on the premise that his IRA compounds at 12 percent a year, which is pretty good.

The second twin procrastinates and doesn't open an IRA until the seventh year—the year his brother stopped. The second twin then contributes $2,000 a year for 37 years. He, too, earns a rate of 12 percent a year. At age 65, they go out for dinner to compare their IRA holdings. The second twin, who is fully aware that his brother stopped contributing 37 years earlier, is confident that his IRA will be worth at least ten times as much.

Nope. At 65, they both have the same amount saved: $1,200,000.

The story blows my mind every time I hear it. The first

brother paid $2,000 a year for six years. If you do the math, you realize he contributed a total of $12,000. The second brother contributed $2,000 a year for 37 years. That means he paid $74,000 — more than six times his sibling — to earn the same $1.2 million.

Bottom line: start saving for retirement now and leave the interest alone to collect interest. What I want to know is why Roy is still cutting hair if he's a millionaire.

The concept has been dubbed the 10-Percent Solution, or Pay Yourself First.

Invest 10 percent of all you earn for long-term growth and never touch it. Not the principal, not the interest. Let it all grow.

My husband has two sons from his first marriage. He constantly tells them and my daughter, Always pay yourself first. Every birthday gift, Christmas present, raise, invest 10 percent. It's a great habit to start with young children and allowance.

It doesn't even take willpower. It just takes a decision to take 100 percent responsibility for your life and your future.

No One Else Is in Charge of Your Happiness. You Are the CEO of Your Joy.

Men cannot read minds.

Every woman knows that, yet too many of them pressure their husbands, boyfriends, and lovers into attempting that impossible feat.

Take Valentine's Day, the most disappointing day after New Year's Eve. How many women know exactly what they want but haven't given their lover a clue? You want a box of Godiva; he buys you edible underwear. You want theater tickets; he takes you to a basketball game. You want a candlelight dinner; he brings home fast food.

Women and men would both be a lot happier if they read their own minds and took care of their own needs and wants.

I spent many years miserable on my birthday, Valentine's Day, New Year's Eve, and Saturday date nights because I had great expectations of what my boyfriend of the month should do to make me happy. The problem was I never communicated what I wanted. Not even to me. Anytime he asked what movie we should see, I shrugged without ever bothering to look up what was playing. Anytime he asked where we should eat, I said it didn't matter, even though I was hungry for Luigi's pizza or Luchita's enchiladas.

Why didn't I just say what I wanted? Because whenever I did have the rare courage to name what I wanted and still didn't get it, I felt devastated. In order to avoid feeling that personal rejection, I kept my wants and wishes secret. If you don't name them, there's still a chance you might get them. It's a strange mind game that women often play, one we almost always lose.

Finally, I learned the secret. When someone asks what you want, instead of denying you have wants, instead of hiding your heart's desire for fear you won't get it, try this: Ask yourself what would truly make you happy. Don't settle for one answer or even two. Think of three options to offer them, all of which you like. They still get a hand in choosing what to give you, but you've stacked the deck in your favor.

When it comes to dating, work, marriage, parenting, and every relationship you find yourself in, you might as well take responsibility for your own happiness because no one else has the power to make you happy but you. Focus your energy on designing the life you want instead of waiting for someone to show up and hand it to you on a platter. Finish college. Establish a career. Figure out what makes you happy and choose it, every day.

It's not up to anyone else on the planet to make you happy. Not your mother, your father, your spouse, your partner, your girlfriend, your boyfriend, your kids, your boss, your colleagues, your friends, or your horoscope. It's up to you and you alone.

It all starts by choosing to be happy.

When you find yourself feeling stuck in fear, doom, and gloom, sadness and self-pity, simply stop and ask yourself this: "Do you want to be happy?"

The answer isn't, "Yeah, but..."

No buts about it.

It's all up to you.

Right here and now, choose happiness. When you find yourself stuck in a mood you don't want to be in, ask yourself: "What would a happy person do right now?" Practice being happy. Act as if you are.

Make it part of your daily and weekly routine to be happy. Make a weekly appointment to pamper yourself. Schedule an hour for you on the calendar. Call it an hour of beauty. An hour of thrills. An hour of peace.

Visualize your ideal day and live it. Wear your favorite outfit. Take a nap. Stay up late. Eat pizza for breakfast. Design a dream day for you and you alone.

Get a massage. Give yourself a pedicure. Go wild. Paint each toe a different shade of red. Buy yourself new underwear. Toss out the panties with safety pins and more holes than a chunk of Swiss. You deserve better.

Call a bunch of friends and have a come-as-you-are party. Ask everyone to bring a chocolate entrée.

Create a sanctuary in your home, a private spot where you can pray, dream, create. Pull a chair up to a window. Hang a fern or arrange a circle of violets. Set out your favorite books.

Curl up and read some love sonnets. Take a bubble bath. Or a steamy one with floating candles. Cut fresh flowers and stick them on the nightstand.

Tickle your funny bone. Watch silly sitcoms, buy some comic books, listen to an old Bill Cosby recording.

Take yourself out on a date. Plan a whole evening with you. Order your favorite wine, appetizer, entrée, and dessert. When the waiter says, "Just one?" Say, "Yes!" with glee, not shame.

Listen to your favorite music from high school. Burn yourself a CD of your favorite songs. Call it the sound track to your life.

Jot down the 20 best things that have happened in your life so far. Then write down 20 things you would like to happen and pick one and do something to help make it come true.

Write a letter to yourself from the person you were at age six. What would the child you were say to the grown-up you are? Use a fat crayon and write with your left hand (if you're left-handed, use your right).

Rearrange your bedroom. Get more sunlight and moonlight into the room. Hang some twinkling lights in a corner.

Eavesdrop on your conversations with you. If they aren't pleasant, change them. Write a new script. Post positive affirmations all over the house. Hide them in the glove compartment, the medicine cabinet, the freezer, the lid of the dryer, the sock drawer.

Gather up all those loose photos and put together an album or collage of the people who truly love you the most.

Take care of your own needs and wants and you won't be foisting desperate expectations on others. You'll no longer go to them hungry for anything. You'll go satisfied, with something to share that will enhance you both.

Accept and celebrate that you are in charge of your own happiness. You are officially appointed CEO of your own destiny. As one friend taught me, you can be happy or you can be miserable. It takes the same amount of effort.

Frame Every So-Called Disaster with These Words: "In Five Years, Will This Matter?"

T ake any so-called problem, disaster, and crisis and ask yourself this: In five years, will this matter?

The answer is almost always no.

Think back to your own schooling. It took me 12 years to finish my bachelor's degree. Does it matter now that it took so long? Nope.

I wanted to be a forest ranger and needed 25 hours of chemistry credit. I flunked the first class. I also got a D in zoology and a D in child psychology. At the time, I saw myself as a failure. It got worse. I got pregnant and dropped out of school. But when I returned six years later, the college had an academic forgiveness policy. They gave me amnesty and erased those grades. Voilà. Instant grade point average leap.

Too often we agonize over the small stuff.

You've got a huge headache or killer cramps or a serious

sinus infection that's making it hard to get out of bed. You spend all night tossing and turning, debating whether to call in sick from work. Call in. In five years, will it matter that you took a day off?

You've got a report due and it isn't perfect. It's the best you can do, but it isn't the best you wanted to do. You wanted it to be ten pages long. It's only nine. Relax. In five years, will it matter?

You've got a baby nursing at your breast and you want to return to work. You want to stop breast-feeding but worry it'll traumatize the baby. Will she feel abandoned? Will a bottle between you destroy the mother-daughter bond? In five years, it won't matter. The important thing is that you love your baby.

My friend's two-year-old was hooked on his binky. That kid sucked it so loud and hard he sounded like a Hoover vacuum cleaner. The pacifier was going to interfere with his growing teeth, but his mom worried how he would sleep without it. Finally, she told him they were going to mail it to a child who needed it more. He got over it in one day, sleeping soundly that night and every night after.

Parents go through it all the time. Their child isn't walking as early as someone else's child. Will it matter in five years if the baby takes his first step at 9 months or 14 months? Either way, the child isn't going to crawl to kindergarten. Same with potty training. Parents freak out that junior is still in diapers at one and a half or has accidents at age two. Relax. No child goes to first grade wearing a diaper.

Try it out on job interviews, dates, and grades. Will this matter in five years? Five months? Five minutes? Probably not.

What about when it's something tougher? When there's more at stake? When it impacts others? The five-year question still works. Sometimes you have to look down the road and ask: What about this problem/situation/incident will matter in five years? One coach did that and taught his team an amazing lesson. It was a tough lesson, but one they'll never forget.

Cincinnati Colerain High football coach Kerry Coombs had taken his football team to 13 victories in 13 games. His boys pounded the last opponent 49–7. His kids poured their hearts into every game and were days away from the Super Bowl of high school football: the state championship. Everywhere he went people congratulated him. All weekend long, it's all he could think about.

Everyone was wild about the big game on Saturday until a graduate of the school was watching TV sports highlights and told his mother, "Hey, I went to eighth grade with that kid. I wonder why he's still in school."

The mother, who worked at the school, asked a counselor the same question. He looked up the boy's record and found out the player failed ninth grade and was in his fifth year of high school. That made him ineligible to play sports. The information was passed on to the coach, the principal, and the superintendent.

No one in the whole world knew that boy was ineligible except four people. It didn't matter that the boy played football for only two years in high school. It didn't matter that the boy had family problems and barely showed up for ninth grade. It didn't matter that his grades were terrible and that he had finally pulled them up, got ten new friends, and was trying to make something of his life.

A rule is a rule. And if the coach reported the infraction to the state, his team wouldn't get to play the big game.

"It wasn't easy," Coach Coombs told me. "I'd be lying if I didn't say there was part of me that said, 'Only four people know about this.' But in the end, I could never have lived with that. That would have been a far worse lesson for our kids to learn, that we knew we did something wrong and didn't tell. I'd never be able to look those kids in the eye again."

The school reported itself to the state. Then the coach called all his football players down to the auditorium. All except one. Another coach drove the ineligible player home to break the news to him in private. The team knew it was serious when Coach Coombs asked them to pray. When he broke the news, they cried. Then he took them out onto the football field to end the season. They stood in their school clothes surrounded by empty seats and threw the football.

He did what every great coach would do. He turned it into a lesson. "Nobody has died, nobody was hurt. Life is going to go on," he told them. "You'll encounter tragedy and disappointment of this kind again in life. The true measure of any man is how he picks himself up off the ground when he's been knocked down."

As the shock waves went through the community, the name of the ineligible player was blasted over TV and radio and in the newspaper. A warrant was issued for the boy's arrest because he hadn't made restitution on a theft charge. He had no money. His coach drove him to the police station so he could turn himself in. The boy was devastated. So was the coach. It was one thing to see a football season end prematurely; it was quite another to see a young boy's life unravel.

"He's had to come such a long way," the coach said. "People lose sight that this is a kid. He may be eighteen, but he's just a kid."

The coaches had been so busy giving the boy rides to school, helping him with his homework, and checking his grades every week, making him feel like he was worth something, that no one ever asked about his eligibility.

What happened next? Food, faxes, and flowers flowed into the school from all over the state. Even officials from other high schools called to offer support. People donated money to help the ineligible student make restitution.

The coach told them no. A coach to the end, he asked for this: "Offer him a job instead."

He turned it into a winning season, one they would remember long after they graduated. He knew that five years down the road, once they were all in college, forfeiting a football season that could have meant a state championship wouldn't be a disaster at all. It would be a lesson about honesty and integrity that would carry them a lot further along in life than any victory on a football field would.

Always Choose Life.

I found the secret of life in tenth-grade English class when the teacher made us read the book *Walden* by Henry David Thoreau.

He wrote about living in the woods on his own for two years and two months. He built a small home a mile from anyone else on the shore of Walden Pond in Concord, Massachusetts. The passage that spoke to me in tenth grade still speaks to me:

"I went to the woods because I wished to live deliberately, to front only the essential facts of life, and see if I could not learn what it had to teach, and not, when I came to die, discover that I had not lived. I did not wish to live what was not life, living is so dear."

The secret of life is to choose life.

Living is so dear.

Four years after reading how Thoreau drove life into a corner, life drove me into a corner. I was a college student of 21 facing a wall of fear. My period hadn't come for four months and a mound was growing between my hip bones.

I didn't want to be pregnant. I tried to pray it away, then simply decided I wasn't pregnant. But denial works only so far and for so long. It actually doesn't work at all to stop a growing baby.

Back then, you couldn't go to a store and buy a pregnancy kit, pee on a stick, and find out in the privacy of a bathroom if you were with child. You had to go to a doctor, give a specimen of urine in a cup, and wait a week for the results.

I took my specimen to a small agency in Kent, Ohio, that specialized in helping unwed mothers. The women at Birthright weren't hostile antifeminists, they weren't crazy pro-lifers who screamed and called people murderers who chose abortion. They simply wanted to help women know that giving birth and keeping the baby or placing it up for adoption were viable, vibrant options.

The day the results were in, I stopped at a pay phone and called the agency for the results. They wouldn't tell me over the phone. Standard procedure, they lied. I walked across campus that day to the small downtown shopping area where the agency was located. My feet didn't seem to touch the earth. I floated there, almost as if I already knew change was acoming.

The woman behind the desk seemed so happy about the news. Even though I should have known, the shock of the words felt like a slap in the face. You're pregnant.

Me? Me who was only 21? Me who was scared and lost and

alone? Me who had ended the relationship with the baby's father months ago? Me who was clueless about what she was doing with her life?

And yet way deep down, like the calm of the eye of the storm, peace filled my center. Life. A new life was growing. Inside of me.

I said yes to it that day and every day since.

At the time, there were two ways to look at it: abject failure, or wonderful opportunity. I ended up dropping out of school, quitting my job as an emergency medical technician because I couldn't lift bodies without risking injury to my back and the baby. I lived at home with my parents and felt like a big-time failure in the world.

But on the inside, in a private world I shared with no one, I felt joy over becoming a mom. I had to keep it secret because the world wants you to be ashamed.

That child, that daughter, that baby I once tried to pray away? Greatest gift in my life. Looking back on all my 53 years, greatest detour life ever gave me.

Choose life.

For me, that isn't a controversial antiabortion slogan. It's a way of looking at every day, at every choice. When I have to make a decision, I ask myself, What is the most life-enhancing choice to make? Then make it.

When I found out I had cancer, the treatment options all looked bad to me: surgery, chemotherapy, radiation. Unfortunately, the doctor suggested all of the above.

I had seen too many people waste away from cancer. As an EMT, I used to drive people to radiation and chemo treatments, people who were too ill to go by car, people on their last breaths. Three of my aunts had died from cancer after years of fighting, after years of suffering. Would that be my fate?

One day, just before I started the chemotherapy treatments that I was dreading, I played a little game. What if I just didn't do it? What if I refused chemo and just trusted that surgery got it all and prayer would protect me? Hmm. I kinda liked how that felt. But as the day went on, deep inside of me, I knew that wasn't choosing life. Not for me. I knew I had to do everything possible to keep this body alive to house my spirit. I knew that God wasn't done with me yet.

In the end, I couldn't shush that whisper, that small still voice that is God. It kept whispering, "Choose life." It reached an operatic crescendo by the end of the day.

And so I did. I chose life. I took the treatments, all of them. They made me sick then made me better. The entire experience transformed my life and the lives of those around me, from my daughter and husband to perfect strangers.

Among the greatest gifts of my entire life, right up there in the top ten — no, in the top five — are two things I never would have picked.

Being an unwed mother at 21. Best thing that ever happened to me.

Being a cancer patient at 41. One of the best things that ever happened to me.

They changed me for good, changed me forever.

Life took me down a path I didn't want to be on, didn't plan to be on. Yet once there, I learned the secret of life is just that: to choose life. Living is so dear.

28

Forgive Everyone Everything.

A blue bumper sticker on my car proclaims, "God bless the whole world, no exceptions."

So far no one has challenged me on it. I confess there are many days when those words challenge me, when I harbor exceptions. I used to have a long list of them. Then it came down to one person. I couldn't let go of that one resentment.

It's easier to forgive those who hurt you than those who hurt the people you love. How do you forgive the father who abandoned your daughter? Who stopped showing up in her life? Who let her down every Christmas and birthday? Who kept making promises he didn't keep?

I had made my amends to him years after she was born. We had dated in college for a few months, then I broke up with him. Months later, I found out I was pregnant. When I told him about the baby, he suggested we get married. I didn't see the point. If we didn't want to date each other, we surely shouldn't marry.

When my daughter turned five, she started asking about her dad. He had never met her. I took a hard look at myself and realized it wasn't my place to cut him out of her life. After weeks of prayer and counsel with a spiritual mentor, I called him one day and invited him into her life. I apologized for having excluded him and left it up to him if he wanted a relationship with her. I needed to clean my side of the street, and I did.

He had moved on and married. He and his wife wanted children but she was unable to have any. He had never told his wife that he already had one. Before he met Gabrielle, I cautioned him: If you open the door to her, you open it all the way. You can't meet her then vanish. This is a commitment, not a curiosity, so be sure it's something you truly want to do. Talk to your wife and think it through. Make sure it's the right decision for both of you.

When he met Gabrielle, he fell in love. He started seeing her every month, then took her for whole weekends. He and his wife treated her like a princess, even made a bedroom for her at their house. For a few years he stayed in her life, then gradually slipped away. She would come back from weekends at his house complaining that he worked the whole time helping the neighbors or the people at his church and she barely saw him. Then he and his wife adopted two girls. In time, the visits, calls, and letters stopped. As a teenager, she worked up the courage a few times to confront him. She called and cried and he promised to stay in her life, but he never did.

I got so angry with him for hurting her over and over. How

hard was it to write or to call? I worried she would grow up blaming herself for his absence, thinking there was something wrong with her, not him.

She went off to college, fell in love, and got engaged. Her fiancé was a human Swiss Army knife, an engineer who loved to hunt, fish, and fix things. They set a wedding date. But eight months before it rolled around, Gabrielle wanted to postpone the wedding. She had just graduated from college and had never lived on her own. She needed time to grow up and into her adult self. Somewhere deep inside she knew they weren't the right match, but she couldn't say it.

One night, it all fell apart. When she asked to delay the wedding, he gave her an ultimatum: now or never. Either they kept the wedding plans or they were finished. After many tears and much heartache, she handed him back the ring. He left and she never saw him again.

It was the toughest decision she ever made. For the longest time she felt raw and fragile. Then one weekend, she attended a retreat on forgiveness. She came back changed. The retreat set her free.

We so often hear that slogan, "Forgive and forget." Most people can't do the latter, and maybe shouldn't, to protect themselves. But what if, instead of forgetting, we retold the story? That's what she learned on retreat. Instead of telling the saga that portrays you as a victim and someone else as a villain, rewrite the script. Instead of justifying and defending your pain, release it for good.

Too often we keep telling the injury story. We get attention and sympathy by being a victim or by being right or by being wronged. We seek cheap payoffs that keep us stuck. If we're invested in someone being our villain, we must love being the victim. We have to let go of both characters in the story.

My daughter had carried within her a story that kept hurting her: Her dad abandoned her over and over. Her fiancé was a great guy who she hurt and abandoned. What if she saw it in a different light?

She started telling herself a new story. Her dad had done the best he could. For some reason he wasn't capable of giving more. It had nothing to do with her. She could no longer take it personally. She couldn't change who he was. Perhaps he couldn't, either.

Neither she nor her fiancé needed to be cast as victims. Theirs, instead, was the story of two people who had loved each other, exchanged gifts of the heart, then set each other free. In time, he found someone else to marry. And she found James, an incredible gift to us all.

The story moved her from grievance to forgiveness to freedom. Forgiveness is giving up all hope of a better past. At first that sounds harsh, but once you let go of what you wanted the past to be, you can start changing the present and create a better future.

I tried it out. The story I always told painted Gabrielle and me as victims. I was the poor, struggling, single mother. Her dad was the villain who abandoned us both. A few weeks before Gabrielle's wedding, I worried that she would feel sad not to have her dad walk her down the aisle. I made a shift in consciousness, and decided to tell a different story, not one of absence, but of presence.

I dug through boxes in the attic and found every picture I had of her dad from our college days. I bought a small scrapbook and sat down with my memories. On every page I stuck in pictures of him and wrote about every good quality he had.

Then I made another scrapbook of all the men in her life who took his place, who filled in the gaps. My own father, my five brothers, my friends who taught her to ride a bike, throw a football, swing a bat. On the front I taped in her birth certificate. Ever since she was born the line for FATHER had remained blank. Underneath that birth certificate I wrote a new story, one that had been true all along. I told her that line was blank not because she didn't have a dad in her life, but because she had so many, their names wouldn't all fit on the birth certificate.

Some say forgiveness is a process. That's true, but it starts with a decision. Once you decide to change your story, you get your happy ending.

When my daughter walked down the aisle, the men who helped raise her, all those surrogate dads who filled in the blanks, surrounded her with love.

And her biological dad? The best of him was there—in *her*.

What Other People Think of You Is None of Your Business.

As a newspaper columnist, I've been called just about everything.

Moron. Idiot. Asshole. Bitch. Worthless bitch. N-loving bitch. Jew-loving bitch. Sometimes I've been called all those in one day. Heck, sometimes in an hour.

Readers constantly insult me through anonymous calls or e-mails:

"You're so completely one-sided." (I write an opinion column.)

"You're a scum-sucking liberal."

"I can't stand you and never read you." (Yet the reader quoted all the paragraphs she hated.)

"You look like a gremlin." ("The car or the alien?" I always wonder.)

"You're sick."

"You're an insult to God."

"You're a disgrace."

"You're so naive."

"You're clueless, ignorant, and arrogant."

My two favorites: "I lose IQ points every time I read your column." And "I don't know what kind of degree you have—but it must have something to do with stupidity!"

The day my editor at the *Beacon Journal* gave me a column back in 1994, he sat me down in his office and tried to talk me out of wanting it. He warned me that I might not really want this dream job. The readers will be downright mean and nasty, he cautioned, they will attack you every way they can.

He wasn't sure I was tough enough to take it. I was sure I wasn't tough enough but said yes anyway.

I would simply buck up and ignore the mean comments. In my short stint as an alcoholism counselor, I once saw a Father Martin movie called *Chalk Talk*. In the movie, the priest told stories to inspire people in recovery. He told one about a woman who had come to him in tears after her drunken husband called her a whore.

"Would you be upset if he called you a chair?" he asked her.

"Of course not," she said.

"Why not?" he asked.

"I know I'm not a chair," she said.

"Don't you know that you aren't a whore?" he asked.

It doesn't matter what people call you, you decide what you answer to. I would simply remember my identity, what I would answer to.

It was tougher than I imagined. Oh, those calls hurt. The shame on you! self-righteous Christians who damned me to hell or prayed for me in ways that didn't at all feel holy.

The columns ran three days a week with my phone number and e-mail address at the bottom. Some saw that as an invitation to dump all their rage from their bosses or ex-wives or deceased parents. The worst calls came in at 2 a.m. after the bars closed.

If the readers don't break you, the annual ritual of journalism awards will. Every year editors submit your work for writing contests. You don't want to care about the awards, but everybody does. The news business attracts people with twisted egos. Newsrooms are full of egomaniacs with inferiority complexes. We have to be great or else we are nothing.

In the sea of journalism, it's easy to get tossed about by the opinions and views of editors, coworkers, sources, readers, contest judges, and your own doubts and insecurities. Every writer has a fragile ego—a huge ego, but a fragile one. We want to be on the front page every day, yet at the same time we are terrified we're no good.

I found the secret to complete freedom from gossip, judgment, criticism, doubt, and the opinions of others:

Humility.

Not humiliation. That doesn't do anyone much good.

I used to not know the difference in those two words until I saw the definition of humility that one of the cofounders of Alcoholics Anonymous kept on his desk. The entire 12 steps of AA are geared to lead one to humility and a life of service to others.

Dr. Bob kept these words of an anonymous author in front of him:

Humility is perpetual quietness of heart.
It is to have no trouble.

It is never to be fretted or vexed, irritable or sore; to wonder at nothing that is done to me, to feel nothing done against me.

It is to be at rest when nobody praises me, and when I am blamed or despised, it is to have a blessed home in myself where I can go in and shut the door and kneel to my Father in secret and be at peace, as in a deep sea of calmness, when all around and about is seeming trouble.

Perpetual quietness of heart. That's what I truly want underneath all those things I think I want. To be at rest when nobody praises me. That is true freedom.

Life is not a performance, a popularity contest, or a conquest for more power, money, fame, toys, glory, clothes, praise, awards, titles, or degrees. At the end, will any of those matter? There's a country music song where George Strait sings that we don't bring anything with us, and we can't take anything back. Like him, I've never seen a hearse with a luggage rack. And coffins don't come with trophy cases.

One way to stay focused on what truly matters is to create a personal mission statement. Not the long mumbo-jumbo boring ones corporations devise and never adhere to, but a personal mission statement upon which you would truly base your life.

I spent a few hours one day in reflection trying to come up with mine. I closed my eyes and imagined everyone sitting around at my funeral. My kids, husband, siblings, coworkers, friends, neighbors. What would I want my life to have meant at the end?

I wouldn't want them sitting around talking about any awards I got for my writing, or that I invested wisely in my

401(k), or that I was a local celebrity. I don't know what they will say after I'm gone, but here's what I hope to leave behind. I found my mission statement, the words I read every morning, in the prayer of Saint Francis of Assisi.

Lord, make me an instrument of your peace.
Where there is hatred, let me sow love;
where there is injury, pardon;
where there is doubt, faith;
where there is despair, hope;
where there is darkness, light;
and where there is sadness, joy.

O Divine Master, grant that I may not so much seek
to be consoled as to console;
to be understood as to understand;
to be loved as to love.
For it is in giving that we receive;
it is in pardoning that we are pardoned;
and it is in dying that we are born to eternal life.

Every day I use that prayer as my compass. It points to True North. True humility. True peace. I am simply a child of God, as valuable and treasured as every other child of God. Not the best, not the worst, and it doesn't matter a whit what anyone thinks of me.

The Passage of Time Heals Almost Everything. Give Time Time.

T he first time I came to the retreat house, I didn't expect much.

The Jesuit Retreat House sits on 57 acres in the middle of Parma, Cleveland's biggest suburb. It's tucked back off the main road, so you could drive past it your whole life and never know it's there.

A friend invited me to come spend a weekend with women who were searching for a better relationship with God. I wouldn't have put me in that category, but my friend did. To talk me into going, she made it sound like a party of sorts, women sitting around sharing and laughing and talking. I packed a swimsuit, hoping it would be like a hotel or a spa with a pool and a sauna.

When we pulled into the long drive, a statue of Saint Ignatius greeted me at the end. Suddenly, it hit me. Whoa. What was I doing spending a whole weekend with women only? I was a single mom and only 25. I didn't want to be a saint or a nun. What was I doing wasting a Friday and Saturday night in a place where there were no men except for priests?

That first retreat was 26 years ago. I've never stopped going back. Every year the priests change, but Gerri is always there. She's a short Polish woman whose laughter and love fill every room of the place long after she's gone home.

Every retreat, I found Gerri and dumped a problem in her lap. She'd listen, "Uh-huh, uh-huh," with a serious look on her face, then stop me to crack a joke to lighten things up. Then she'd look me in the eye, or try to, being all of four feet nothing, and give me a string of advice that always ended with this kicker:

"Sometimes you just have to give time time."

What the hell did that mean?

Give time time?

I didn't have time. I was a single mom on a mission: find a husband for me, a father for my daughter.

Back then, my problems always had to do with a man who didn't love me enough, which at the core had to do with a dad who didn't love me enough, which at the core had to do with a God who didn't love me enough. Gerri knew that kind of wound takes a long time to heal, and that it heals in layers, not all at once. Gerri's remedy was time. I wanted something faster.

The healing service might be it. I saw it listed on the schedule and the woman who brought me to the retreat house insisted I go. At first I cringed. I pictured a TV evangelist beckoning, "Feel the warmth of my hand," touching my head then screaming, "Demons be gone!" and people dropping to the floor and flailing around like guppies out of water mumbling words that not even God would understand.

I didn't want to go. Mostly because I was scared of God. And scared of my wounds. I'd covered them up for years. Why go ripping off the Band-Aids? Father Benno Kornely, who wrote the healing service, seemed so inviting, though. So I sat in the chapel as Father Benno played soft gentle songs about how much God loves us. Good thing he set out tissues. I went through a whole box before the first song ended: "I will never forget you, my people, I have carved you on the palm of my hand."

Me? God has my name on that palm? Regina Maria Frances Brett?

The tears cleansed the wound. I came back every year, sometimes twice a year. Every healing service healed another layer of the wound. It took me ten years before I got through the whole service without crying.

Father Benno's words took us through a journey of our memories. He invited us to let surface whatever needed to be healed. He walked us through our lives, healing the blows we felt or delivered to brothers and sisters, teachers and classmates, neighbors and relatives. He prayed that we be healed of all that hindered our love and happiness. He pronounced us a new creation then invited us for the laying on of hands. No hocus-pocus, just a blessing on our palms with oil that had been blessed.

We came forward and carried in our hearts what we wanted healed. Every year, every healing service, mine was pretty much the same: the dad wound. My dad was the most powerful man in my life, for good and for bad. He was the most generous, selfless, thoughtful person I have ever met. He was also an angry belt-waving rage-o-maniac I dreaded.

It took years of counseling to get to the bottom of the pain. Then came the spiritual work. I didn't know how to heal the relationship, to get back to having one. I alternated between being afraid of my dad and being angry with him. Love found no entry. I didn't feel any more anger for him, but I still couldn't feel any love. I wasn't even ready to ask for help to love my dad. I wasn't that willing yet. But I did constantly pray, "God, help my dad know how much *You* love him."

I knew intellectually that I loved my dad. I hurt him, he hurt me. Neither of us meant to. We both did our best, but sometimes our best is terrible, mine included.

During that five years of missing out on Christmases, Easters, anniversary parties, birthdays, and births of new nieces and nephews, I wanted to go back home, wanted to be part of my parents' lives again, but I didn't know how.

Then one day, I heard my dad had been diagnosed with lung cancer. Doctors gave him six months to live. Two days later, I ran into my friend Ruth. Without knowing my situation, she started talking about her mother, how God had given her the grace to be with her mom as she lay dying. All of a sudden, all my fear lifted. It was like a window opened that had always been locked. I knew it was time to go.

I drove over the next day to visit my dad. His hair was white and soft as angel hair. He grinned and chattered and then grew too tired to talk. He seemed absolutely joyful that day as he stood in the doorway and waved to me. I'll never forget that wave. I never saw it again.

Three days later, he ended up in the hospital. He struggled

to breathe. I sat by his side as he coughed and hacked. My dad didn't smoke. He had worked in basements fixing furnaces, basements with asbestos hanging off pipes he bumped up against all those years ago. I patted his back and told him thanks.

My mom sat silent and still in a chair, shaking her head. She knew he wasn't coming home. So did I. I held his hand, caressed it, and without words told him how much I loved him. As I sat there, my heart filled with love at all the times he had been so nurturing and tender with us when we were sick with the flu.

He slipped into unconsciousness the next day. It was only a matter of days. I lit a candle in my room and prayed that God would either heal him or quickly and gently take him home. Dad would never have wanted to be in a nursing home. He was 83. He had had a good life. As the candle burned, I imagined his three deceased sisters, like angels, bearing him up, carrying him home.

He died while the candle was still flickering. The next day I drove to my mom's. I stopped and bought food, as my dad taught us to do. My mom forgave me for my absence in their lives with these words: "Would you write his obituary?"

I got to tell the whole world what a great guy he was. For years, I had put the magnifying glass on the pain, now I got to put the magnifying glass on the gifts, and there were many.

Gerri was right all along. When the healing came, it was complete and made me feel whole.

Time needed time.

No Matter How Good or How Bad a Situation Is, It Will Change.

My friend Mena has a saying: "Life is rough, wear a helmet."

Boy, she isn't kidding.

Some days you feel like you need one to survive the ups and downs, the twists and turns, the jostles and jolts and sudden brakes. And that's just the morning rush hour traffic.

The secret is not to get too attached to any of life, good or bad. The good times will come and then they will go. The bad times will come and then they will go. Our job is not to cling to one or to fight the other but to allow them both to teach us and polish us.

There's an old saying people use to cope through bad times. "This too shall pass." Most people don't want to use that when it comes to the good times. We don't want them to pass. We want them to last forever. But sooner or later, everything changes.

The secret is to ride life like a raft in a river and let it carry you through the white water and the still water and beyond. Float on down like a leaf, holding on to nothing, trusting the flow of the river.

The first time I went white-water rafting, a guide gave us a lecture on the dangers of the river. If you fall out of the raft, do not try to stand up, do not try to grab on to a rock, do not try to fight the river. The river will win. If you fall out, relax, point your toes downstream, tuck your head to your chest, and let the river carry you. It will always take you to calm water. He gave us each a paddle and told us to listen to his directions as we entered each set of rapids. Then he told us to remember that people really do die out there so be careful, and have fun. Oh, and he had no helmets for us.

That lecture sounded comforting and clear in the safety of the spot of grass where the rafts and life jackets were stacked up, that is, until he mentioned the dying part. We figured he was joking until we heard the pounding of the raging river downstream and there was no turning back.

That first time white-water rafting, I had no idea what to expect. The Youghiogheny River churns into Class III and IV rapids at Ohiopyle, Pennsylvania, and makes for an exciting ride around rocks, ledges, and wild swirling currents. I sat on the edge of the giant black raft, which felt like a big dopey inner tube. There was nothing to hold on to. The four of us steadily paddled into the rapids, but once in them, it felt like someone had turned on a washing machine.

The river bounced us up and down, right and left, under water and high above it. I tried to paddle but wasn't sure if my oar was in the river or in the air, I was spinning around so quickly. It was wildly and wickedly exciting. Until I fell out. My first instinct was to try to stand up or grab on to a rock. Bam! Smack! Ouch! Oh yeah, what was it that guy said about relaxing? I made a feeble attempt to point my toes and tuck my head but I couldn't even find or feel my toes in that cold swirling river.

My contact lenses were floating in my eyes so I couldn't see ahead of me. My life jacket was too big and kept bobbing up to my ears. I had to use my hands to pull down on the shoulders. The paddle got swept away. It was hard to figure out when to take a breath. I couldn't see anything but water around me and above me. I couldn't hold my breath any longer or swallow any more river, so I said, God, if you want me to live, do something fast. I'm Yours. Right then I felt someone yank me out of the river. Another raft had come by and they grabbed me by my life vest and saved me. By the time we got to still water, I was ready for more.

The last trip I took down the river, I went with a group of people who were too bold or too cheap to hire a guide. We rented a raft and hit the river.

Big mistake.

We rode the river daredevil style, aiming at rocks and hydraulics, almost daring it to hurt us. We rented life jackets and set out to conquer the river on our own. We brought food and a rope for safety. But there was no one to tell us how to approach each rapid, no one to warn which boulders to avoid, so we galloped through one set of rapids and slammed into and onto a rock. A rock the size of a Chevy.

We were stuck on that boulder, couldn't move an inch,

with white water churning all around us. When we threw our weight to one side to try to twist our way off the rock, the raft overturned. The raging water pinned me against the rock, pounded into my chest so hard I could barely breathe. The others somehow pulled me up onto the rock. By then, the raft was long gone.

What now?

Two guides from another group came by in kayaks. They told us to jump back in the river and let the water carry us downstream. I thought they were joking. We had no other option. The kayaks and other rafts had no room for strays. One by one, my friends said good-bye, jumped in, and floated away. I was the only one left. The guide in the kayak kept urging me back in the water. I didn't want to give up the security of the rock, but the river wasn't going to stop for me that day or any day.

Finally, he promised to follow me down in his kayak, so I said a prayer, slid off the rock, and floated away to calm water. I have never forgotten that day, how sometimes you have to give up the security of your rock for something better.

I once read an interview with Pastor Rick Warren, who wrote *The Purpose Driven Life*. What he said reminded me of that river:

> Life is a series of problems: Either you are in one now, you're just coming out of one, or you're getting ready to go into another one. The reason for this is that God is more interested in your character than your comfort. God is more interested in making your life holy than He is in making your life happy.

He talked about the lesson he learned in the greatest and toughest year of his life. That year he made millions on his book but his wife got cancer.

I used to think that life was hills and valleys—you go through a dark time, then you go to the mountain-top, back and forth. I don't believe that anymore. Rather than life being hills and valleys, I believe that it's kind of like two rails on a railroad track, and at all times you have something good and something bad in your life. No matter how good things are in your life, there is always something bad that needs to be worked on. And no matter how bad things are in your life, there is always something good you can thank God for.

Then there's the female NASCAR driver who said: "Life is like a racetrack. It's the curves that make it worthwhile." Easy for her to say. She gets to wear a helmet to work.

Regardless of the analogy, life is a wild, wonderful journey. Chaos will come, calm will follow, and then it will start up all over again. The secret is to savor the ride.

All of it.

Your Job Won't Take Care of You When You Are Sick, but Your Friends Will. Stay in Touch with Them.

There is something about turning 40 that makes people want to celebrate by decorating with black balloons and sending cards that graphically detail bald heads, wrinkled faces, sagging breasts, and protruding bellies. Forty seems to be the halfway point between here and death, the beginning of the end of life as we know it.

With that in mind, I had no idea what to give the man in my life for his fortieth birthday. Bruce was acting 60, questioning the worth of his life up till now, taking stock of what he had accomplished, rating himself as a father, a businessman, a citizen.

All I could think of was how many friends he had collected in 40 years. That seemed to be a better measure of his life than his income or community status.

The image of George Bailey from the movie *It's a Wonderful*

Life kept coming back to me. George Bailey, who never saw himself as a success, got a chance to see what the world would have been like without him. The moral of the movie was that no one who has friends is a failure.

I wanted Bruce to reflect on the friends he had, not on his body's odometer turning or the roads not taken. So I asked 40 people to write a letter sharing how he had touched their lives. How had he changed them, molded them, moved them?

They were to send the letters to me to be wrapped all together and presented as a gift. The project sounded easy at first: Just call 40 people. Just write one letter. But as the old saying goes, writing is easy — just sit down and open a vein. "This is more like opening a ventricle," one letter writer said.

Everyone agonized. A few called each other and asked, "What are you going to write?" as if they could borrow something. It was a delicate assignment, one that would expose both writer and receiver. Some opted to joke about turning 40, others used humor to express their love. Most of them ended up saying what is most difficult to say in person, what is often never said in person.

As the birthday grew closer, the letters trickled in. Two came by Federal Express, a half dozen by fax, and one by e-mail. One man dictated his over the phone. He said he didn't know how to express his feelings in writing and would leave it to me.

I covered a sturdy box with pages from a 1954 *Life* magazine and stuffed the letters inside. When the day came, we went out to dinner and a movie and had dessert with a handful of friends. Afterward, Bruce expressed relief about how well the day had gone. Then I handed him the box.

As he shuffled through the cards, he looked confused. I explained what they were. He looked stunned. He looked at the return addresses on the envelopes but didn't open any right away. When he did, the emotion poured out of him and the letters. He laughed so hard he cried. He felt so moved he wept.

In all, 40 people performed open-heart surgery on Bruce. They opened up lines to his heart that had been closed, or narrowed with time. They brought up the past, the days of black-light posters, long hair, hitchhiking, and rock concerts they were all too stoned to remember. They thanked him for late-night phone calls, last-minute advice on getting a job, long talks about how to survive divorce.

The mother of one of his closest friends wrote a lovely poem. One woman designed her own card. One man wrote his on sheet music. Bruce plans to pass the letters on to his sons one day so they will know what his life was about. That it was more than the money he made, the business he owned, the woman he loved. It was about the friends he made and kept.

"Most people don't ever get to know how people feel about them," he said, wiping away tears. "This is the kind of stuff they say at your funeral."

That is why I tell the story of that gift. Too often we don't hear what we mean to others until it is too late. Too often we don't know what to do for others until it is too late. When I first learned I had cancer, I worried about missing work, about missing volleyball games, about preserving all the commitments on my calendar. The nurse struggling to set up my first chemo appointment shook her head and said, "You need to get your priorities straight." She was right.

Work took a backseat. Cancer didn't take the front seat. My friends did. They took the driver's seat.

Sheryl held a chemo shower. Friends brought earrings and scarves and hats. Beth picked up the tiny harmonica earrings Sheryl bought me and played "The Chemo Blues." Judy came over and washed my hair. Other friends brought me stacks of movies to watch, bought me slippers and pajamas. Countless others sent cards, meals, and inspirational books.

My job? The newspaper somehow got printed on the days I was too sick to write. That world kept turning without me. My friends? They kept my world turning.

My friend Marty always says that if you've got your friends and your health, you've got everything you need. Cancer taught me that if you keep your friends high on the priority list, even if you lose your health, you'll still have what matters most.

Believe in Miracles.

T he doctor tried to break the news as gently as possible.

"You know how when you're little and you ask for a pony, you pray and hope for it and you never get it? Well, this is that same type of situation. Sometimes you don't get the pony."

The doctor was trying to tell Chris Wood's parents that the situation was hopeless, even beyond their prayers.

Chris was 21 and stationed in the navy in San Diego that June of 1989. After an afternoon of drinking at a Padres game, he fell out of a pickup truck on the way home when the driver switched lanes.

After Chris landed on the four-lane highway, a car hit him. He bounced into another lane and was hit by another car. Luckily, the next vehicle to come along was an ambulance. Chris had a broken pelvis, jaw, elbow, and knee. He had massive head injuries and tire marks across his back.

For the next three months all the news on Chris from the doctors was bad news: *He will not live... he will be a vegetable... he will never walk... he will never have a meaningful life.*

His family back in Akron started prayer chains. One night his sister was awakened suddenly. She says it was God who whispered to her these words: "He will live and not die and proclaim the mercies of God."

From then on, that was the family's mantra.

It got Chris through 32 surgeries, a three-month coma, and years of treatment at the Veterans Hospital in Cleveland where he goes for rehabilitation. At 29, Chris had the same bright blue eyes and sandy hair as before, but everything else had changed.

His speech is slurred, as if he's been drinking. The breathing tube damaged his vocal cords. The head injuries slowed his thinking. His face turned crooked from his jaw healing incorrectly. A purple zipper scar runs up his left arm, which dangles at his side. He must concentrate to be able to open his hand.

Chris is a walking hardware store. There's a screw in his elbow, a brace on his leg, a hinge in his knee, and a plate in his head. His brain no longer works the same. He used to excel at math but now struggles with the basics. When he enrolled at Kent State University six years ago, he got D's and F's even in the simplest classes. One of his rehab workers urged him to drop out.

He gave it some thought. "My mind would say, *You're wasting your time*," he told me. But instead of listening, he would turn to his favorite Scripture passage, Proverbs 23:7: "For as he thinketh in his heart, so is he."

"It means what you believe is what you're going to be. If

you think you are second and a failure or number one and front of the line, that's what you will be," he said.

He credits his mother for his successes. Linda coached him along using the Bible as her playbook. Chris now has three jobs: he interns at Edwin Shaw Hospital working with head injury patients; he does computer design work for Living Water Fellowship Church in Akron; and he is an usher for the Akron Aeros baseball team.

It took three tries to pass his driver's test, but he finally got his license. It took six years of therapy, but he put away his wheelchair and can now move with a walker.

He still struggles to come up with the right words when he talks. He pauses, squints hard, trying to force his brain to remember how to work.

It works fine enough. On graduation day, Chris Wood gave a commencement address without saying a word. He walked across a stage at Kent State University and picked up his bachelor of arts in psychology to a standing ovation.

He wasn't the smartest one there.

He wasn't the most talented one there.

But he was there.

His mother never lived to see it. She had died the previous June of a heart attack. But she lived long enough to know that the doctor who said it was too hopeless to even pray was wrong.

That doctor got a postcard from Chris's dad letting him know how it all turned out.

It simply said, "We got the pony."

34

God Loves You Because of Who God Is, Not Because of Anything You Did or Didn't Do.

To mark the new millennium, the pope reintroduced indulgences, a kind of amnesty for sinners popular in the Middle Ages. Basically, indulgences are a way to earn brownie points with God before Judgment Day.

Call it a shortcut to salvation, a way to shave time off your sentence in purgatory, the place where Catholics were taught souls go to be cleansed before arriving in heaven. Indulgences, which people once paid for in cash, were long ago banned by the Catholic Church. Back then, sinners bought their way out of purgatory, sort of a fire sale before the fire.

The new indulgences would carry no price tag, just a heartfelt act of sacrifice and penance. Acts of penance and sacrifice are noble when offered solely out of love for God or others, but it seems there's something selfish about doing them to reduce one's time in the clink, so to speak. Besides, can you really earn your way to heaven?

Almost every priest knows the sermon about the man who dies and meets Saint Peter at the pearly gates. Peter tells him he's got to get clearance before he's admitted.

"What does it take?" the man asks.

"You need at least five hundred points to get in," Peter tells him.

"Well," the man says, "I was a dedicated husband, father, and employee. I never cheated on my wife, my boss, or the IRS."

"Hmm," Peter calculates. "That's good for a hundred."

"A hundred! That's all?" the man exclaims. "Let's see. I gave money to United Way, volunteered weekly at a soup kitchen, rang the Salvation Army bell every winter, and spent a week's vacation every summer building houses for the poor in Central America."

"Okay," Peter says, tapping away on the calculator. "You're up to about three hundred fifty."

The man panics. He can't think of any other great deeds or sacrifices he did to make up for the deficit. He'll never get into heaven.

"That's it," he says sadly. "I throw myself on the mercy of God."

"You're in!" Peter says and throws open the gate. "Welcome home."

The story is a comforting one. Instead of dwelling on God's justice or on our sacrifice, the focus is on God's mercy.

A Persian mystic named Rabi'a wrote what it meant to truly love God: "O my Lord, if I worship you from fear of hell, burn me in hell. If I worship you from hope of Paradise, bar me from its gates. But if I worship you for yourself alone, grant me then the beauty of your face."

Years ago, I took myself to the Abbey of Genesee in New York to get unstuck. I had a good relationship with God but felt like there was still a huge stumbling block I kept tripping over. No matter what I did, no matter what good works or intentions or sacrifices I made, it never seemed good enough. I never felt good enough.

Deep down I still didn't feel worthy of God's love. What would it take to really and truly believe in my core that God loved me, as is?

I signed up for confession and met with Father Francis. He wore the white robe and black cowl of a Trappist and seemed humble and holy enough. Instead of giving him the confessional laundry list of sins, instead of rattling off a grocery list of how many times I lied or gossiped or envied another, I got down to the core. Underneath every single defect of character in me, my envy, my resentments, my fear, is this: I'm not enough, I told him.

The monk sat and smiled. His whole body swayed in a nod like he truly understood and had been waiting for this brilliant shining moment to share his most holy profound truth. I sat back and waited for a deep revelation to flow forth. Instead, he started to tell me the story of the Prodigal Son. "There was a man who had two sons..."

My heart sank. I already knew that story. The monk was all excited, like he'd just heard the story. He relayed it detail by detail, in slow motion. He was so intrigued that the one son had taken his inheritance early and squandered it on wine, women, and song, then decided to come crawling back to his father and be treated at least as well as a servant.

The son returned, but before he even had the chance to apologize, the father was so happy to see him, he ran to greet him and hugged and kissed him. The son objected, said he was no longer worthy to be called his son, but the dad threw the best robe on him, a ring, shoes, and announced to everyone to kill the fatted calf and start a party.

Yeah, yeah, yeah. I had heard it all before. The monk loved the part I always hated about the faithful son who never strayed. That son was out in the field working when he heard the music and dancing. He grew angry that he'd been faithful all along and never disobeyed, but his brother who strayed got a party. Right about then I realized I had picked the wrong monk. I wasn't going to get a Zen koan that would change my life or a Buddhist mantra that would realign my heart or a Thomas Merton quote that I could hang my life on forever more.

Nope. All I got was a rerun. When he got to the end of the story, the monk grinned over the punch line. The father told the faithful son that all he had belonged to the son, and that he would get his due, but they should all rejoice that the lost son had been found.

The monk's face glowed. Mine darkened. He was siding with the wrong son. What did this have to do with me? The monk repeated the ending. The son didn't have to apologize. He didn't have to make amends. All he had to do was turn to his father. Turn to his father. That was it. That's all it took to come back. That's all any of us need to do.

"God loves us because of who God is," the monk said. "Not because of who we are."

At first it stung hard as a slap in the face. Did he just insult me?

Then I felt that zap to my heart. The kind where it feels as if an arrow has just pierced it, an arrow shot straight from the bow of God to the bull's-eye of you.

God didn't want my perfect offering. God didn't care if I became the best writer in the world or the humblest servant or the greatest volunteer since Mother Teresa. God didn't care if I screwed up big-time or left a mess in my wake as long as I turned back.

God loves me because it's God's nature to love.

I can't earn that love. I can't lose that love.

I was enough not because I was enough, but because God is.

I am home free.

So are you.

Whatever Doesn't Kill You Really Does Make You Stronger.

Cancer and I met the day I woke from a surgical biopsy on February 19, 1998, to a new life. Everything before that fell on the other side of the time line of life: B.C. Before Cancer.

I wouldn't let cancer kill me. Not if I could help it. The first year was a blur. By the time I recovered from surgery, it was time for four rounds of chemo. By the time my hair was starting to grow back, it was time for six weeks of radiation. By the time I got my energy back, I was into year two. That's when it hit me. Damn, I had cancer.

Trials and tribulations like cancer and divorce or loss of health, income, or loved ones can either kill you or make you stronger. Cancer made me stronger after it knocked me to my knees over and over again. During those months of treatment, I faced terrible moments of despair when I wanted to give up.

In the end, cancer made me tougher. Sinus infection? Flu?

Pulled muscle? No problem. My attitude now: Pain? So what. Fear? Who cares. I used to be scared when I wrote my column. What others call writer's block I call page fright. All the doubt and insecurities would beat me up. Now, no more hedging, no more tiptoeing. I speak up with no regrets, no fears, no holding back. If I don't say it now, when will I?

My daughter constantly reminds me why it's important to talk about surviving. It's an obligation we 10 million cancer survivors in America share. Every day somebody new gets the verdict. The first thing you do is cry. Then you ask questions for which you might not want to hear the answers: Is it curable? Is it treatable? Has it spread?

What you really want to know is this: How long will I live? No one knows.

I gave it my all. Surgery. Chemotherapy. Radiation. And more surgery. I had both breasts removed after learning I carried the BRCA1 genetic mutation that increased my chances of getting breast cancer up to 87 percent in my lifetime.

What is it like to be breastless?

Audrey Hepburn is my inspiration. I have a newfound admiration for gymnasts and ballerinas. I can sleep prone without any lumps or bumps between me and the 300-count sheets. I can go braless *and* breastless. I can be a B, C, or D cup or no cup all in the same day. I can exercise, jog, or jump rope without a sports bra strangling me. I will never sag or fear the effects of gravity.

If I had known how easy it was to live without breasts, the decision to have a double mastectomy wouldn't have been so hard to make. Looking back, it was the toughest decision I ever made in my life. Once you have your breasts removed, there's no going back, no what-ifs, no bargaining, no negotiating, no more delays or denial. It's final. You are the only one who can make the decision and the only one who has to live with it the rest of your life. It's so permanent and scary and drastic.

And then one day it isn't. It's just who you are now.

For the first year, I felt raw. Physically and emotionally. A part of me was gone.

We live in such a breast-obsessed culture. It seems like every famous woman has had implants. You can't escape cleavage even at the grocery store checkout. It's a virtual breast fest on the covers of *Cosmopolitan*, *People*, and *Us*. For the first year, I couldn't walk into a Victoria's Secret. I couldn't bear to be bombarded by breasts and by bras I could no longer wear.

Right after the surgery, I couldn't wear prosthetics while my chest healed. It felt so strange to have a flat chest. My cushion, my padding, my shield was gone. I felt exposed and vulnerable. I missed my breasts. Every so often in a bubble bath I'll gather the suds and pile them up on my chest and try to remember what my breasts looked and felt like. In time, I've forgotten what they felt like. Forgotten them, in a good way. I no longer compare the old me and the new me. I'm just me.

Every so often my breasts want me to remember them. Phantom sensations come and go. Sometimes, out of the blue, it feels like my breasts are back, I can feel their weight. I reach under my bra just to check. Nope. Still gone.

I wear fake breasts most days. Instead of implants, I got inserts. It's strange having a doctor write you a prescription for breasts every two years. They cost $300 each but insurance covers most of it. They're filled with silicone. They wiggle and jiggle like breasts and slide into the pocket of a mastectomy bra.

The women I talked to before surgery who wore fake breasts told me to make the prosthetics part of you. That was tough at first. They felt hot and heavy and fake. Then one day, I was running down the steps and I felt them bouncing like real breasts. Just like my old ones. We became friends that day. I named my fake boobs Thelma and Louise.

They feel soft and natural when I hug people. They're perpetually perky and don't flatten out when I lie down. But I'm still nervous around cats and brooches and corsages. I'd hate to spring a leak.

The prosthetics let me look curvy, for me, for Bruce, and for my clothes to fit better. When I don't wear them, I'm so flat that people ask if I've lost weight.

Before surgery, I read that many women choose to get reconstructed breasts because they don't want a constant reminder of having had cancer. Good for them, but I don't see my flat chest or my fake breasts as reminders of cancer or loss.

Being a woman has so little to do with a pair of mammary glands. What makes me a woman is the size of my heart and the shape of my soul. You don't need breasts to be a woman, a mother, a wife, a sister, a daughter, a niece, an aunt, a grandmother, a godmother, a writer, a friend, a lover. But you need to be alive to be all of those.

No, I am no less a woman. In so many ways, I am more of a woman now than ever before. I got to the core of who I am, past the shell, to the center. I am closer to the heart of me. Literally. My heart no longer hides under the cushion of a breast. It is closer to the world, and I am closer to what makes me me.

It's up to me to decide who I am, how I look, what it means

to be sexy or feminine or pretty or powerful or successful or happy apart from what anyone else says.

This chest is my blank canvas, my blank page. I can write anything on it.

I no longer cry in the shower, no longer cringe when Bruce touches my bare chest, no longer care about how I look. I gave up my breasts to be here. When I look at my blank chest, I see life. That flat chest reminds me every day that I chose life, and I should get on with the business of living it.

I don't feel any less a woman. I feel like Wonder Woman.

Our job as survivors—of disease, of divorce, of grief, of despair—is to bear witness, to carry the torch of hope for all who journey through the valley of the shadow of death and out again. It's up to those of us who get to see the view beyond that valley to share it. Life from a survivor's point of view looks pretty damn good every day.

Am I in remission? Who knows? I got the wake-up call and I'm not going back to sleep. If I had to do it all over again, I would. I'd do whatever it takes to get more life out of this body. Life is worth the fight.

Am I cured? All these years of life say yes, but I look at it this way: I got a daily reprieve. And I'm not wasting a minute of it.

Growing Old Beats the Alternative.
Dying Young Looks Good Only in Movies.

Whenever I call to say hi and ask my friend Ed, "How are you?" he always gives me the same answer: "I'm old."

It's never a complaint, just a fact. The older he gets it's a boast.

It doesn't bother him to be on the other side of 50. His dad died from heart disease young. Ed has the same approach I have to getting older: bring it on. He beat heart disease; I beat cancer. We aren't stuck growing old. We GET to grow old.

I love the picture in a magazine ad of old ladies frolicking in a pool. They're all wearing bright hats and silly grins under a headline that reads, "You're only old once."

Turn 50 and Hallmark dresses your birthday in black and declares you over the hill in cards, banners, shirts, balloons, and stickers. Turn 50 and you're officially an antique. Not me. When I turned 50, we celebrated big. Getting cancer at 41, I never imagined reaching that lovely landmark that is 50.

In honor of that most magical age, here are 50 things to do when you turn 50.

1. Sleep through it.

2. Spend $50 on yourself.

3. Read aloud Dr. Seuss's book *Happy Birthday to You!* and see what they do in Katroo where they sure know how to say happy birthday to you.

4. List 50 places you've never been to and see them before you turn 60. Not just faraway exotic countries, but local museums, churches, back roads, ponds, and parks you've never visited.

5. Start writing the book you've always wanted published. Write the first 50 lines.

6. Plant a tree to honor your youth.

7. Visit a cemetery and give thanks that you're still on the right side of the grass.

8. Sign up for a class to take solely for fun.

9. Drive 50 miles on back roads you've never been on before. Don't take a map and don't check your GPS. Let the road lead you.

10. Blow 50 bubbles out your bedroom window.

11. If someone asks you what you want for your fiftieth birthday, name 50 things you've always wanted.

12. Pick one new volunteer activity and donate 50 hours to it this year.

13. Sprinkle 50 pennies around the world today to bring 50 people good luck.

14. Think you're over the hill? Find a good-size one, roll down it, and scream, "Youth is wasted on the young! Youth is wasted on the young!"

15. Take a pin to your birthday celebration and pop all black balloons.

16. Celebrate wrinkles. Buy a box of raisins and savor every one of them.

17. Take a 50-minute hike in the woods.

18. Plan an imaginary 50-day vacation. Don't let your pocketbook limit your fantasies.

19. List 50 people who have made their mark on your life.

20. Call everyone you love and tell them.

21. Write yourself an advice letter from the person you will be at 80 years old to the person you are now at 50.

22. Walk around in private in your birthday suit for 50 minutes, marveling at how it still fits after all these years.

23. Send 50 thank-yous (by e-mail or real mail) to all those you love.

24. Vow to meditate 50 minutes a day, 25 minutes every morning and 25 every evening.

25. Write down 50 wishes for the future—small ones and big ones, wild ones and tame ones—put them in a jar, and don't read them until your next birthday.

26. Reflect on all the people you've lost in 50 years and the gifts they gave you.

27. Reflect on all the people who are left in your life after 50 years and the gift they still are.

29. Eat 50 M&Ms.

30. Name the one thing in your life that makes you feel young and embrace it more deeply.

31. Name the one thing in your life that makes you feel old and change it.

32. Spend 50 minutes thanking God for the first 50 years of life.

33. Rent the movie *It's a Wonderful Life.*

34. Donate $50 to your favorite charity.

35. Hold a baby close today.

36. Hold the hand of an old person.

37. Play 50 minutes of your favorite opera, jazz, or country.

38. Leave a 50 percent tip for a waitress who served you breakfast, lunch, or dinner.

39. Sing your favorite childhood song in the shower.

40. Read 50 pages of your favorite classic.

41. List 50 words that describe what you absolutely love about life.

42. Honk your horn 50 times today to let the world know it's your birthday.

43. Be still and watch the clouds for 50 seconds.

44. Make a list of all 50 states and check off all the ones you have seen and star the ones you haven't.

45. Say good morning to the sun and good night to the moon.

46. In 50 words or less write what you plan to give to the world around you in your remaining 50 years.

47. Stare at the sky until you can count 50 stars, then kiss them all good night.

48. Turn out the lights, crank up the stereo, and listen to Louis Armstrong sing "What a Wonderful World."

49. Blow out 50 candles and make a wish for whoever needs it most.

50. Instead of counting sheep, fall asleep counting off all the things you are grateful for, starting with birthdays.

Your Children Get Only One Childhood.
Make It Memorable.

When you're a single mom, every date turns into a job interview for the position of father and provider. I was spending way too much time and energy turning myself inside out to make every guy I dated want this package deal that was us. It wasn't working. I was in the midst of finding Mr. Right.

If only... I found the right father for my daughter. If only... I found the right husband for me. If only... he came along, then we could be truly happy. Meanwhile, I was neglecting my daughter's needs and wants. By trying so hard to find her a dad, I was forgetting to be a mom. It became crystal clear the day I took her to a huge party and lost track of her while I was flirting with yet another guy. The band announced from the stage they'd found a missing child. The reality? I was a missing parent.

I was working at an alcohol treatment center when I was 26

and Gabrielle was 4. I met a woman who worked with troubled adolescents. She told me the biggest message she'd like to give every single mom is to stop worrying about career and finances and partners and futures and focus on their children right now.

"Your children have only one childhood," she said.

If she had it all to do over, she said, she would have held off on dating and just dived into being a mom 100 percent. I hated those words at the time. They poked at my guilt button labeled single mother. If I could find my daughter a dad, then we would be complete. We would be a family. I spent way too much time dating, way too much time agonizing over each Mr. Wrong who drifted into and out of our lives. I introduced my daughter to way too many guys, had them spend the night, dragged her through the Days of Our Lives that my life became.

I don't recall that woman's name, face, or job title, only her words. They burned me like a brand and left an everlasting imprint on my life. She shook my world when she told me parents should put their children first. She said, "You have your whole life to date, to find a career, to meet the man of your dreams. Your children get one childhood. Make sure you're there for it."

I carried a load of guilt being a single mom. I didn't have the money to take my child on vacations to Disneyland, or anywhere for that matter. But over time I realized that my daughter didn't need vacations to be happy. She didn't even need a dad to be happy, although I wish I could have provided her with one. She needed one adult to be a full-time parent, 24/7.

I learned to be present and make each day joyful and

meaningful instead of trying to construct some future dream of happiness by ignoring the needs of the day we were in.

When I look back on my own childhood, past the rocky moments to the most meaningful, memorable ones, it is the small stuff that I still carry in my heart.

The Halloween that my dad grabbed a bedsheet then snuck around the houses in the dark and walked up the sidewalk to our house and knocked on the door. At six foot two, he was the tallest trick-or-treater we'd ever seen. As soon as we handed him the candy, he yanked off his ghost costume, and every time he told the story, he couldn't stop laughing.

The moments my mom stood by the kitchen sink humming or playing Perry Como, the Mills Brothers, Mitch Miller records and trying to get us to sing along. Or grabbing one of us to do the polka with her in the living room.

Then there was Grandma's wave. My grandma lived on a farm. She wore support stockings, an apron over her dress, and hid her gray bun under a babushka. She cleaned other people's houses for a living. She kept a lollipop drawer filled for our every visit. She spoke broken English, sprinkled with Russian, Slovak, and maybe a tinge of German. She couldn't even pronounce my name. She called me Virginia. Every visit we each got our own tiny glass bottle of Coke and a bagful of the greasiest, saltiest chips. We loved it. She introduced us to abundance. She didn't have much, but she turned that little into a feast. And whenever we left, Grandma stood at the end of her driveway, a driveway lined with gladiolus she carefully planted and dug up and replanted year after year. She waved and waved and waved until we were out of sight.

I'll never forget that wave.

My daughter is grown now, and the fond moments we recall are just that—moments. Before she married, I created a scrapbook and filled it with the best memories.

The day we sailed plastic ducks in the rain during a downpour. We raced them down the side of the curb in the rainwater running into the storm sewer. We got soaked and laughed ourselves silly.

The day we took a cafeteria tray and went sledding at the end of the driveway on the mountain of snow the city plow left behind. In college, I stole the orange plastic tray from Kent State University when I was a student. We carved pumpkins on it. We served food on it. That tray brought us more joy than any gift I bought her.

The Sundays we read the comic strips out loud with different voices, making the Mary Worth comic strip more dramatic than *Macbeth*.

The nights I made up stories before bed that didn't always make sense because I would fall asleep halfway through Peter Caterpillar.

The Barbie dream house I made out of boxes and odds and ends and Contact paper better than any house Mattel ever made. I glued small corks on the corners of a pencil tray to make a bathtub. I cut up a washcloth to make towels and rugs. I turned a metal Band-Aid box into a clothes hamper, a cigar box into a canopy bed, old check boxes into a refrigerator and stove. She wore it out.

The skateboard she was too afraid to stand on and rode sitting down in the house, sailing across the wood floors of the duplex we rented.

The video scavenger hunts she organized with her high

school friends. The time I drove her and her friends out at midnight to paint the huge rock in front of campus.

The Shel Silverstein poems we read aloud and memorized about the polar bear in the Frigidaire and the girl who didn't get the pony and why you should always, always, always, always, always, always, always, ALWAYS sprinkle pepper in your hair.

The Halloweens we turned our front yard into a cemetery with cardboard whitewashed graves marked Ben Dover, Al K. Holic, Willy Makeit, Betty Dont.

The Saturdays we pounded down junk food from Lawson's and took random road trips without a map on country roads over the surrounding counties.

The concerts we splurged on and laugh about now: Milli Vanilli, MC Hammer, Debbie Gibson, New Kids on the Block, and Vanilla Ice, Ice Ice Baby.

We laugh about how little we had, and yet how we ended up having it all. Just not all at once.

The husband came along. The career came along. Everything I wanted came along, once I put first things first.

The truth is, you can have it all, but you might not get it all at once.

38

Read the Psalms. No Matter What Your Faith, They Cover Every Human Emotion.

If it were possible to do an autopsy of the soul, what we'd find would be 150 parts, each one reflected in one of the Psalms.

"All the sorrows, troubles, fears, doubts, hopes, pains, perplexities, stormy outbreaks by which the hearts of men are tossed, have been depicted here to the very life," wrote John Calvin. He called the Psalms the anatomy of the soul.

Even when the Psalms are chanted in Latin they soothe my spirit. Even when I don't know the words, my soul recognizes them.

For years the only psalm I knew by heart was the only one everyone knew by heart. Psalm 23: "The Lord is my shepherd, I shall not want." I printed it on memorial cards at the funeral home where I worked.

It's easy to remember and never fails to comfort. It's easy to picture that sheep up on the hill, lost and frightened. The story always has a happy ending, the Good Shepherd seeks and finds it and brings it home. Who can't relate to feeling lost in the valley of the shadow of death? It shocked me to find out there really is such a valley. When I was on my honeymoon in Jerusalem years ago we stood in the hot sun on a roadway looking at a huge expanse of land spread out below us.

"What valley is that?" my husband asked our guide.

"Yea, though I walk through the valley of death," our guide began to chant.

It takes more than Psalm 23 to get me through life. The entire Book of Psalms tells the story of the journey every human being walks in life. The 150 psalms speak of wonder, joy, and celebration, but also of the dark night of despair, desolation, and abandonment. Places we find ourselves too often.

The Book of Psalms addresses every facet of the spiritual journey, the ups and downs, heights the soul ascends, depths to which it falls. The Psalms offer praises as well as curses, consolation, and desolation, boasts of strength and cries of weakness. Mostly, they make me feel less alone.

On my worst nights of despair, when I can't even remember a single line from a single one of them, I clutch the entire book to my chest like a child would a teddy bear. Only then can I sleep. I bought my Book of Psalms from Genesee Abbey where the Trappist monks end every prayer praising "the God who is, who was, and is to come at the end of the ages."

I took a class on the Psalms in graduate school, a class taught by a Jewish rabbi. Professor Roger C. Klein of Temple-Tiferth Israel in Cleveland told us that we didn't have to be scholars to understand the Psalms. We didn't need great intellect, he said. "It just requires a soul."

The Psalms reveal the many faces of God: powerful rock, shepherd, companion, comforter, provider, host, creator, judge, advocate, and deliverer. My favorite? I like the idea of a personal God of joy. I pray often, "You are my strength and my song."

The Psalms address every sort of inner and outer turbulence from crop failure to enemy attacks, from illness to loneliness. All of them were meant to be sung, and if they were, it would be like hearing an opera of the Bible.

I once read that President Bill Clinton read the entire Book of Psalms to find spiritual relief from the political pressures facing him. It's easy to see their appeal, no matter what your religion. They cover everything:

For poverty there's Psalm 10: "Lord, you hear the prayer of the poor; you strengthen their hearts."

Campaigning is covered in Psalm 35, which speaks to battles with the opposite party: "O Lord, please my cause against my foes; fight those who fight me . . . vindicate me, Lord, in your justice do not let them rejoice. Do not let them think: Yes! We have won, we have brought him to an end."

Any employee could use a dose of Psalm 56: "Have mercy on me, God, men crush me; they fight me all day long and oppress me . . . all day long they distort my words."

Spouses can rely on Psalm 141 for restraint: "Set, O Lord, a guard over my mouth; keep watch, O Lord, at the door of my lips."

The Psalms are now the bookends to my day. I'm drawn to monasteries where they run like a pulse through all who chant them. The nuns at Mount Saint Benedict Monastery in Erie, Pennsylvania, start each day with the same one: "O God, come to my assistance. O God, make haste to help me." The monks at the Abbey of Gethsemani in Trappist, Kentucky, end every day with the same words, "I will lie down in peace and sleep comes at once, for you alone, Lord, make me dwell in safety."

The Psalms sometimes find me. I once walked into a restaurant where a group was holding a prayer breakfast. There, on an easel near the door, someone had dissected Psalm 46 down to its smallest, deepest core. All that was left was the distilled essence of every prayer:

Be still and know that I am God.

Be still and know that I am.

Be still and know.

Be still.

Be.

39

Get Outside Every Day. Miracles Are Waiting for You to Discover.

One Tuesday morning in September I left the house for a long walk. When I came back, the world had changed forever, or so it seemed.

When I came home, six messages blinked on the answering machine. I played the first one and heard my husband's voice, broken by grief, urging me to call right away. He sounded as if there were a death in the family. The rest of the calls were from family members telling me America was under attack. The last one was from my sister in New York City, saying that she, her husband, and my godson were safe in their Brooklyn apartment watching flames eat at the World Trade Center towers.

I turned on the TV. The towers were burning. The towers were falling. The towers were gone. People ran for their lives like in a Godzilla movie. Cars melted. Rescue workers scrambled under a cascade of rubble. Smoke hid the Manhattan skyline. The Statue of Liberty looked feeble and small, as if she held the white flag of surrender instead of the bold torch of freedom.

For days I sat at the TV and watched the attack over and over, as if each time the results might be different and those towers would stop short of falling.

For a few weeks, nothing felt the same. I couldn't even go for a walk. I was afraid to do what I was doing that Tuesday when the world went mad. It made no sense, but I was afraid that if I went out for another walk I'd upset the delicate balance of life and come home to the same sort of messages.

When I finally did get back outdoors, it felt like the world had righted itself. I walked through one of Cleveland's Metroparks and watched the leaves. The leaves still floated carefree as ever from the sky, leaving behind naked trees that prayed with arms raised high in quiet hallelujahs.

The leaves didn't know that everything changed on September 11. The wind blew them fast and low, sending crowds of them skittering across the ground like joyful schoolchildren set free for recess. When the wind blew hard and high, the leaves tumbled like confetti on the tree-to-tree carpet of the forest floor. When the wind blew gentle as a whisper, solitary leaves performed somersaults, backflips, and triple axels.

In the woods, America was not under attack, nor was it at war, frightened of anthrax, or celebrating a rebirth of patriotism. The only battles pitted squirrel against squirrel over precious acorns. The only danger of contamination came from touching leaves of three or from stepping in the piles horses left behind. The only red, white, and blue on display were fat red berries and tufts of white seed parachutes that floated against a clear blue sky.

In the country of the woods, life continued its surrender to death to bring forth more life. The cycle of life went on, uninterrupted. Nature is so durable. It reminds us that we are, too.

Henry David Thoreau wrote of going into the woods because he did not wish to live a hurried life nor did he wish to practice resignation. His words bore new meaning. I went back into the woods because I did not wish to practice resignation, did not wish to give into fear over anthrax, anger over terrorists, despair over a crippled economy. I went into the woods because it felt less scary to walk alone in the woods than to sit at my desk and open the mail or turn on the TV and listen to pundits.

On any given day, if you want to escape from all the madness, personal or worldly, leave the TV, the computer, the iPod, put on your sneakers, and take a hike. There's always a surprise. Along one five-mile hike, I watched a man try to photograph his Irish wolfhound against a waterfall. The dog was too obedient to cooperate. Every time the man with the camera called the dog's name to get him to look up, the dog ran over to him.

On another path, I surprised two napping deer, witnessed a blue heron come in for a landing, and stood in a marsh full of cattails watching those tall corn-dogs-on-sticks sway in unison like gospel singers praising the Lord.

I passed miniature waterfalls and read quotes carved into the wood railings and found this message by Rachel Carson to encourage and comfort all who passed: "Those who dwell among the beauties and mysteries of the earth are never alone or weary of life."

How true. The year I had cancer, I remember going for a walk in the snow. It was March and I had just been diagnosed. I was dreading all that lay ahead, surgery, chemo, radiation. The snow distracted me, swirled in my face, pulled me into the dazzling, dizzying present moment. I looked up and felt the flakes pound me like feathers from a pillow torn open from above. I savored every touch, and knew I was not alone.

In his journal, Henry David Thoreau wrote of the home and church that nature provides:

Alone in the distant woods or fields, in unpretending sprout-lands or pastures tracked by rabbits, even in a bleak and, to most, cheerless day, like this, when a villager would be thinking of his inn, I come to myself, I once more feel myself grandly related, and that cold and solitude are friends of mine. I suppose that this value, in my case, is equivalent to what others get by churchgoing and prayer. I come home to my solitary woodland walk as the homesick go home. I thus dispose of the superfluous and see things as they are, grand and beautiful.

40

If We All Threw Our Problems in a Pile and Got a Look at Everyone Else's, We'd Fight to Get Back Our Own.

W henever Father Clem Metzger gives a retreat, he never fails to tell the story of the woman who wanted a new, improved self.

The middle-aged woman ends up injured in a car accident. Paramedics rush her to the hospital. As she floats in and out of consciousness, she begs God to keep her alive. God tells her not to worry. God promises her a long, long life. It isn't her time to go.

While she's in the hospital recovering from her broken bones, she figures she might as well get a few other things done. She opts for a tummy tuck and, oh, why not get the breast augmentation? She has her eyes lifted and her nose reduced. She looks and feels like a new woman. She's so pleased with her new body and young face, she can't wait to show the world.

Minutes after she leaves the hospital for home, a bus rounds the corner, slams into her, and kills her. When she gets to heaven, she's furious and tells God, "You said I was going to live a long life. What happened?"

God studies her face and says, "I didn't recognize you!"

The first time I heard it, I laughed at the woman, but not at myself. It took a few retreats for the truth of that story to sink in.

Every so often, I want to borrow someone else's life. I take a sneak peek at some other woman's journey and want to try on her shoes and walk around in them. I stare at my feet and compare my shoes to hers. Hers look prettier, sexier, hipper, and way more comfortable. Of course, I have no idea how those shoes actually feel on her feet, only how I think they would look and feel on mine.

It's easy to compare my insides to other people's outsides and come up short. Every so often I get a blunt reminder of how my problems are really my greatest gifts.

A few years back, I attended a function of hundreds of movers and shakers in Cleveland. I felt intimidated surrounded by a roomful of powerful mayors, congress members, business executives, and judges. They all looked smarter, richer, and more important than I'd ever be.

One judge came up to me to talk. She was a bright, rising star in the community. She asked me if I had children. I took out the photo that I keep tucked in my wallet of my daughter in her wedding gown. The judge studied the picture of my daughter sitting next to me in that poof of white tulle. Her eyes grew misty. "I don't have any children," she whispered. "I had five miscarriages. I wanted a child so badly. I can't imagine what it's like to have a daughter."

She touched the photo to her cheek and closed her eyes, as if to soak up the kiss of motherhood, an imprint she could feel but never experience.

Every time I look at that picture, I feel newly blessed.

Most of us are walking around blind to the gifts that we have been given until we see the problems others have endured. My friend Michael Brittan is a prominent attorney who could very well be the happiest person I've ever met. Some find him to be annoyingly happy. He's constantly smiling, praising others, pointing out the good in every bad situation, living in awe of every speck of beauty around him. He's like a human firefly. He absolutely glows.

Those who don't know him see the suit and tie and assume he's had an easy, cushy life. They don't know the backstory. Michael's dad lived on the wrong side of the law. He ran some gambling operations for the local Irish mob, the Celtic Club. The Italian and Irish mobs had a war going on in Cleveland. Michael's dad shot and killed a man during a high-stakes poker game a week before Michael started law school. A few months after he got out of jail, while Michael was still studying law, his dad was murdered. It didn't hold Michael back. If anything, it propelled him forward.

Michael became a lawyer, and years later became president of the Cleveland Metropolitan Bar Association. He volunteers in the Cleveland schools teaching the three Rs—rights, responsibilities, and realities. He goes to inner city schools to promote a positive attitude toward the legal system and to help kids finish high school. He tells them they can succeed with the right mental attitude, a definite purpose, and the willingness to work hard. Despite the chaos of his life while he was in law school—dad on trial for murder, dad in jail, dad murdered—Michael set a goal, worked hard, and graduated first in his law school class.

How can some rich white guy in a suit and tie relate to a room of poor black teens? He can relate to the pain, heartache, fear, and insecurity many of them live with by having a dad who lived a life of crime. He shares his wounds.

There are all kinds of people like Mike in the world. On my annual weekend retreats at the Jesuit Retreat House in Cleveland, I constantly discover that we're all broken, just in different ways. After seeing the scars of others, I embrace mine with gratitude.

On one particular retreat, I was feeling freshly wounded by life. As I walked around the 50 acres, I noticed a doe limping through the woods. She had smooth walnut brown fur and took delicate, slow steps. When I stepped closer, I noticed she walked on three legs. One front leg had snapped and swung in the air.

Oh, my heart sank. I prayed she wasn't in pain. I stood and cried for that deer. How fragile she looked. I named her Bernadette and prayed for her the whole weekend. I would never forget her. The other deer I couldn't tell apart, but this one I would always remember. I would know her by that broken limb, by her wound.

And as I walked on through the woods, I couldn't shake the image of her brokenness. Then it struck me. That is how I often feel on the inside. That is how God knows us, by our wounds.

Saint Augustine once wrote, "In my deepest wound I see

Your glory and it dazzles me." To God, they are not wounds at all, but gifts.

Someone once said that God comes to us disguised as our life. In the mess of that life, in the problems and flaws we'd like to wish away and pray away. Taped to my daily planner is a quote from Thomas Merton, who reminds me that I was formed perfectly with all my imperfections.

Merton was a Trappist monk, poet, and social activist who died in 1968 after spending most of his life in prayer and solitude at the Abbey of Gethsemani in Kentucky. He believed that we all have a unique destiny, a purpose that matches each of us alone. God has never repeated it and never will in any other person. That uniqueness is driven home for me by the prophet Isaiah, who says in the Bible that God called us from our mother's womb, formed us uniquely, and will never forget us. He has carved my name, and yours, on the palm of His hand.

I must give to God what he cannot receive from anyone else: the gift of me.

Yes, if we all threw our problems in a pile, I'd take mine back, not because they are easier, but because they are mine. My lessons. My honors. My gifts.

Don't Audit Life. Show Up and Make the Most of Now.

Leslie Hudak had a poker-chip theory about teenagers. She believed that everyone is born with a certain number of chips. Some children lose their poker chips along the way from insults, criticism, and poor parenting. By the time they get to be teenagers, they have to hoard what little they have left, so they can't afford to take risks or to trust people.

She was a high school English teacher who made it her job to keep giving kids more chips. She bought a can of gold spray paint and painted poker chips in her driveway. She handed the gold coins out to teenagers at Kent Roosevelt High School where my daughter was a student. Leslie zeroed in on the bruised kids, the problem kids who needed encouragement the most. As they built their piles of chips they could gamble: Try out for a play. Go out for a sport. Ask someone to the prom. Dream big.

Leslie took the biggest gamble. She could have simply done

her job as a teacher and gone home every night feeling content. Instead, she cosigned car loans for students. Leslie bought them lunch. She helped pay their rent. She gave her old car to a student who needed one to get to work. When one boy wanted to try out for pole-vaulting, Leslie watched videos on the sport and became his coach.

She would show up at a home with a bouquet to thank a student, host huge spaghetti dinners at her place, deliver Easter baskets and sacks of Christmas gifts to kids who had nothing.

She decorated the girls' restroom to get the girls to stop smoking at school. She spent a weekend putting up flowered wallpaper and fresh paint and set out baskets with free hair spray, tampons, hand lotion, and candy. It worked. The girls loved all her changes and guarded that room like sentries. No one dared smoke there again.

When she heard about some of the teens' life stories, she stocked refrigerators with food, taught girls to do laundry, and held the hands of girls delivering babies without partners and parents to help.

And it was Leslie who was there on their wedding days, helping girls into bridal gowns, girls who had no moms around to celebrate. She believed in their dreams. One girl wanted to be a singer, so Leslie gave her money to help her record a CD.

That student sang "Amazing Grace" at Leslie's memorial service. Leslie died in a car accident on her way home from school one February day. She was 58. Thousands showed up to mourn. The student Leslie legally adopted ten years before, a boy who had grown up in foster homes and had nowhere to go when he turned 18, was listed as a survivor in her obituary.

Everyone at the funeral had a Leslie story. They talked

about how she threw hard candies to construction workers, chatted with bored tollbooth workers, awarded angel medallions to tired waitresses.

When she got frustrated that term papers were coming in late, she dressed up in a pink gown and tiara to address the class as Princess Procrastinator. When she heard that a group of boys was going hunting, she invited all 20 of them over to her house, served them food, and had them watch *Bambi*.

Leslie taught everyone around her not to audit life. When you audit a course, you don't take it for credit, so you barely show up and don't invest yourself 100 percent. Leslie showed people how to make life count as if every moment were being graded, as if every encounter mattered.

She could have stayed in the small box labeled teacher and been satisfied by her work in the classroom. But she would have sold herself and all those kids short. We all have that same choice. Stay in the small box others put us in by job title, income, education, and IQ. Or we can expand the box or leap clean out of it.

Leslie leapt higher and farther than most of us do. She gave her life away. For years she stayed up until 2 a.m. grading papers. Her daughter, Megan, told me, "I don't think my mom watched television in ten years. She gave a piece of herself to everyone, but we never got shortchanged."

Her students, including my daughter, eulogized her as a friend, a teacher, a mother who had the world's largest heart. The last time I saw Leslie, she told me, "I'm always distressed when people expect the worst from people instead of expecting the best. Sometimes we sell young people short."

Every day she gambled on them, she won. And so did they.

42

Get Rid of Anything That Isn't Useful, Beautiful, or Joyful.

Getting rid of things goes against my genetics.

My Depression-era parents kept everything. Having spent their childhood poor, they taught us never to throw anything out. Dad's garage was a temple to thrift, Mom's basement a shrine to saving. Socks with holes? Use them for rags. Shirts with stains? Wear them under sweaters. Jeans with worn knees? Cut them into shorts.

Open my closet door and you can see the family resemblance. What stops me from cleaning it is that I bump into all the me's I left behind.

The Athletic Me can't part with the kneepads, volleyball shoes, Rollerblades, ice skates, and assorted sports bras that convince me I'm still young enough to be the athlete I never was.

The Hip Me owns a black spandex skirt that looks great until I've worn it for three hours. It stretches to hug the derriere but doesn't tighten, so when you stand up it looks like you're hiding twin first graders under your skirt.

The Younger Me used to look perky as a cheerleader in the gray miniskirt with the pleats in the front. Time to let go of that and the $80 shoes with the four-inch heels that feel like I'm wearing stilts on ice.

The Sexy Me believes that one day I will look exactly like the woman on the Black Velvet billboard if I wear the black velvet padded bra or the black stretchy slip that won't let you exhale.

The Nostalgic Me hangs on to every item with a story, like the Bride and Groom baseball caps we got as a wedding gift. Can we keep wearing them? We still feel like newlyweds. Or the hot pink tunic I wore when I met the man I married. He claims it was love at first sight. Thank goodness love is blind.

The Realistic Me takes over and decides it's time to part with anything I haven't worn in five years. I pile everything to give away. A mountain range forms. I feel like a new woman. My life is organized. Well, at least my closet.

A few years later I tackled the whole house after clutter coagulated and clogged the arteries of our home. Saint Benedict once wrote that the extra clothes you store in your basement, attic, and closets belong to the poor. I'm not so sure the poor want dozens of pink fund-raising T-shirts from all those walks for the cure, but they've got them now.

For three months, I was a woman possessed, decluttering the house from top to bottom. It all started with tossing out two nasty chairs. A mustard yellow office chair and an Early American Ugly dining chair. When I put them on the curb one day I found out the neighbors were having a house sale.

Figuring I had a built-in audience, I unloaded our basement onto the curb. I tossed an old coffee table, skylight, rocking chair, stereo, and the green antique marble lamp I picked up off someone else's curb. All it needed was a cord and plug to work, but after a year sitting in the basement, it wasn't any closer to working, so out it went.

My neighbor grabbed it. Fifteen minutes later, it was back on the curb. His wife refused to let it in the house. It turns out one man's trash isn't always another man's treasure. Sometimes it's still trash.

I threw out mismatched gloves and socks, moth-eaten hats and scarves, candles that melted in storage, and fabric for a dress I pinned to a pattern 20 years ago. I didn't even stop to save the pins.

As I sorted it all, I asked myself four questions: Is it useful? Is it beautiful? Does it add meaning to your life now? If this item were free at a garage sale, would you take it? That last question served as a truth serum. Most everything got tossed.

I filled the curb and strangers emptied it. By noon, it was all gone. The house felt ready now. For what, I would find out as time went on.

Decluttering forces you to let go of the past. It creates an opening for the future. What are you making room for? New ways to experience leisure and romance, creativity and serenity. New hobbies, new friends, new goals. Once you evict the excess, you can embrace the essentials: that which is beautiful, meaningful, and enhances your life.

When you finally let go of the person you used to be, you get to discover the person you are now and the person you want to become.

43

All That Truly Matters in the End
Is That You Loved.

For years I wrestled with God.

I always got pinned, then crawled back in the ring for another round.

In between matches, I faked piety and tried oh so hard to be good but could never be good enough. Some people have a Santa Claus God. I had a bogeyman God.

The roots of my misunderstanding with God go way back. Prenatal. I felt like the poet who wrote "I was born on a day God called in sick." I used to believe God wasn't aware of my birth at all. I had slipped by unnoticed and spent the rest of my life trying to get His attention to no avail.

That's when I wasn't cowering in mortal fear, which might have been half an hour on a good day. And good days were rare.

My conscious awareness of our battle started back in

Catholic school or, as I call it, boot camp. In my eight-year tour of duty at Immaculate Conception School in Ravenna, Ohio, first grade scared me so badly I went home for lunch one day and begged my mom not to ever send me back. The first-grade teacher was probably only 20-something and never wanted to teach 46 kids who didn't know how to tie their shoes, blow their noses, or count to 20. Sister P was cruel. We should have been issued Purple Hearts instead of holy cards. When one girl accidentally tore the cover on her phonics book, Sister P wailed at her and knocked her out of the desk and onto the floor. When a child wet his pants, she made him sit in the hall in his underwear. When we struggled to understand addition and subtraction, she screamed at us and called us all devils. One day I wiped my runny nose on the sleeve of my white Peter Pan collar blouse and she called me a pig in front of the whole class for that felony.

I was only six.

This was my entry into the world of school. I had never been to kindergarten. My parents didn't send me.

In second grade, I got a nice nun. Sister Dismas was all smiles and sunshine. Then the next year, the dreaded Sister D showed up in third grade. The first day of school we were to cover our books with paper bags. I didn't know how, so she smacked me over the head with it. The book, not the bag. The next two years, God had mercy and sent me a few lay teachers, non-nuns. A sweet Mrs. Adkins in fourth grade and a friendly Mrs. Plumstead in fifth, whose breath smelled of minty Certs. Then in sixth grade, back to the jungle. Sister E nearly strangled a girl during lunch recess. The girl never came back. In seventh grade, Mr. S made the bad boys stand in front of us all, arms stretched out at their sides as he stacked encyclopedias on their open palms until the boy's laughter turned to tears. One day when I cried, he demanded I look up at him. I couldn't because snot was running down my nose. He barked at me to grow up.

If we girls forgot to bring a hat or scarf to church, the nuns pinned pieces of toilet paper to our heads, as if God would be less offended at seeing Charmin than hair. Once inside the church, we had to face Sister B, the clapper. She clapped once, and we dropped to one knee and genuflected. She clapped again, and we rose to sit in the pew. Act up, and we got clapped across the head.

Where did Jesus fit in to any of this? Jesus was a mere history lesson. A scary one. God loved us so much that He sent His Son to save us. But God, who allegedly was a loving father, let His only begotten Son hang from nails on a cross in the rain wearing nothing but a rag and a crown made of thorns. Think I'll pass on that, God.

How do you please a God like that? Who would want a God like that? Jesus was a course we studied and His Father a bully I could never please.

Then I met Joe.

At first I mistook him for the gardener. He wasn't wearing his Roman collar that day and didn't look much like a Jesuit priest or any kind of priest, for that matter. He stood at the door of the retreat house wearing a red flannel shirt and work pants. He had a big hook nose you could hang a coat on. His cheekbones jutted out like wings from his face. His back had a hairpin curve that made it impossible for him to ever sit comfortably in a chair or ever sleep on his back. Father Joseph Zubricky was the hunchback of the Jesuit Retreat House.

He became the light of my life.

Joe gave us a talk about the God of his understanding, whom he called Jesus. Only it wasn't at all like any God I'd ever heard about. Joe was in love with God and knew God was in love with him. He didn't let religion get in the way of that. Joe, one of God's most twisted, bizarre creations, Joe who had every reason to resent his lot in life, all 206 twisted bones, only loved.

After his talk, I confronted him in the hall. He let me dump all my baggage in his lap, all my arguments against the Church, all my confusion about who Jesus was or wasn't, all my resentments about the nuns and the Church and God. Was there such a place called limbo? What about purgatory? How could I believe the pope, a mere human, was infallible? Joe just smiled. He wasn't going to argue. He waited patiently until I finished ranting.

He said the rules, the dogma, the Church hierarchy, none of that mattered. He could see my exasperation, but his warm brown eyes filled with light, a light that came from the inside. He smiled like a man in love.

"Look, at the end of it all, God is going to ask just one question: Did you love? Eh? That's all that matters. Did you love?"

End of debate.

End of wrestling match.

God 6. Regina 0.

Pinned for good. Pinned by love.

44

Envy Is a Waste of Time. You Already Have Everything You Truly Need.

Uncle Al was dying.

The doctors diagnosed it as pneumonia, but I think his heart finally wore out.

Uncle Al missed the light of his life. He was 81 and had spent most of his life loving my aunt Chris. He never stopped loving her, even when she forgot him, when the Alzheimer's washed away her every memory of their 56 years together. Death wasn't strong enough to part them. He walked around the house carrying a picture of my aunt after she died. He talked to her. Prayed to her. Sang to her. The songs brought her back.

I stopped for a brief visit when he ended up in the hospital with pneumonia. I tiptoed into the ward, a specialized care unit where he had a tiny room all his own. His body took up so little space on that bed, it was lost in the tubes, monitors, and gizmos. He lay flat on his back, his daughter at his side. She looked like his young bride, Chris.

As soon as I said hello, he bolted upright as if I'd used a defibrillator. His thin white wild hair was all askew. He was so skinny, his bones stuck out of the hospital gown, jagged like weapons. I could see my uncle struggle, the pain, the shortness of breath, the difficulty swallowing.

But his mind, it was sharp as ever. He talked for two hours. He started talking and couldn't stop. Uncle Al loved to tell stories. His favorite one was how he met my aunt. He proposed to my dad's sister during midnight Mass. He told me tales about his trips to California, New York, and Chicago. He gasped for air between stories and cities. His daughter kept asking him to pause to breathe.

I sat on his bed savoring every detail as he recalled those years gone by. Then he started singing and wanted us to join in: "Come home, come home, ye who are weary come home," he sang, then smiled.

When we got to the end, like a little kid, he begged, "Let's sing it again."

Every so often a doctor or nurse would come in to remind him to keep breathing the oxygen. He threw them out. He wasn't worried about dying, wasn't interested in prolonging his life. My uncle was ready to go, ready to be with his wife. His wedding vows went beyond "until death do us part."

"I've had a great life," he said through the oxygen mask over and over. "No one has had a better life than me."

What a great claim to make on your deathbed.

To wrap your arms around the life you lived and give thanks for it alone. No regrets. No what-ifs. No should haves.

Uncle Al knew that happiness is a choice. How can you be happy? You choose to love what you already have. Happiness isn't in the raise we want. In the retirement portfolio we build. In the mansion and Mercedes we'll be sitting in if we win the lottery.

Studies show that extra money will not make you extra happy. No one wants to be poor, but once basic needs for food, shelter, and education are met, the extra money you can spend doesn't buy happiness. That's the word from happiness researchers — yes, there really are such things. Those economists and psychologists who are paid to study happiness came out with a report that ran in *Science* magazine in 2006. It showed people with higher incomes didn't report being happier. They reported being more anxious and angry.

Around the same time, a report came out in the newspapers that said having children, being retired, and owning a pet don't affect happiness. It's your outlook — which you yourself choose — that determines whether you are happy.

How to be happy?

Experts offer these tips: Choose time over money. Meditate and pray. Make peace with the past. Spend more time socializing with friends. Seize the day, the moment, the Oreo. (Okay, that last one was my tip.)

People used to turn to spiritual directors for the answer. Nowadays they turn to life coaches. My money is on the monks. Years ago I went on retreat at the Abbey of Gethsemani. A monk had posted a sign outside the room where he was going to give a brief speech. He posed three questions and gave his answers:

Who am I?

A child of God.

What do I need?

Nothing.

What do I have?

Everything.

That sums it up.

Who lives it? Too few of us. One of the greatest models of living it was Mychal Judge, the popular Roman Catholic priest who died in the attacks of September 11. His friend, Father Michael Duffy, a friar from Philadelphia, said this in his eulogy:

"He would say to me, 'Michael Duffy'—he always called me by my full name—'Michael Duffy, you know what I need?' And I would get excited because it was hard to buy him a present or anything. I said, 'No, what?'

"'You know what I really need?'

"'No, what, Mike?'

"'Absolutely nothing. I don't need a thing in the world. I am the happiest man on the face of the earth.'"

So was my uncle. Were they happy because they had everything? Or because they needed nothing? Both.

Happiness isn't getting what you want. It's wanting what you already have.

My uncle Al had it all because what he had was all he wanted. At his funeral we sang his favorite song to him, "All who are weary come home." We all smiled. We couldn't really grieve. We knew he was happy. He always was.

The Best Is Yet to Come.

I once heard of a mother who would cook a great meal, watch her family enjoy every bite, then, before anyone cleared the table, announce, "Hold on to your forks! The best is yet to come."

She was talking about dessert. The same could be true of life.

For most of my life, I rarely counted on dessert. Growing up, dessert showed up on holidays and birthdays, rarely after a Monday through Friday meal. Meat and potatoes were the mainstay. Always potatoes. Dad bought them by the hundred-pound sack. My mom did her best to transform them into interesting meals to feed 11 kids. My dad gave us a roof over our heads; my mom, clean sheets on the beds and three square meals. There was no tucking us in to bed, no lullabies, no frills. There was little time to get to know her.

When you have a big family, you get loved as a group. It's

a different kind of relationship when you have to share your mom with five sisters and five brothers. We didn't have the kind of bond where you go shopping together or get manicures. We didn't have that buddy-buddy relationship many mothers and daughters have. We had the kind of relationship I was still sorting out after nearly 50 years as her daughter. It wasn't a bad relationship. It was a blank relationship.

The things other women miss after their mothers pass away are things I never quite mastered even with my mom still alive. I have loved her clumsily for years. I was now an adult so the failings were mine, not hers.

Part of me wanted it to get better. Part of me had stopped trying. For decades I had waited for her to make the first move. I had waited most of my life. Was I supposed to repair the relationship? Or was she? It wasn't really broken. It's as if it never fully developed in the first place.

Over the years I asked others about it, counselors, spiritual directors, monks I consulted on retreats. I described our lack of a relationship. They all gave me the same advice: accept the relationship you have. You don't have to have a close relationship with your mom.

But everyone else had one. Was there still hope for one?

My friend Suellen suggested that I make a gratitude list. How Oprah, I thought. Suellen said it would have a profound effect. Focus solely on the good that your mom did, and list everything, no matter how small.

I started with being grateful that she gave me life, that she kept me and fed me. From there, I went blank. So many kids came after me — six — I had gotten lost in the shuffle.

Every so often I would add a few things to the list, but for the most part, the list frustrated me and became a painful reminder that my mom wasn't in my life. Finally, I stopped adding to it.

Then my mom's birthday rolled around. The big 75. My sister in Columbus was hosting the party. It was my job to bring Mom, to drive her the two and a half hours. I froze inside. What would we talk about for that long? On some level we were strangers. I wasn't even sure what to buy her. I didn't know her taste in jewelry, clothes, or music. The day before the party, I still hadn't picked out a gift.

So I gave her the gift a writer gives. I wrote.

The night before the party, I dug out that list and sat down at my computer. I stayed up until I came up with the 75 things I loved about my mother. I counted all my siblings, which gave me ten instant items. The more I typed, the more that empty well in my heart filled up with memories big and small. Some made me laugh, some made me cry. When I finished, it was 3 a.m. I printed it out and rolled it up into a little scroll and tied a ribbon around it. I also printed out a list from the Internet of all the major events of 1930, the year she was born. Then I designed a certificate for a day's shopping spree and wrapped that up.

The next day I bought a small plastic crown at the toy store so she could be the Queen Mum for a day. I wanted her to feel special and wasn't sure she would. Birthdays were always so difficult for her. When I was growing up, Dad handed us money to buy her something and no matter what we picked out, it always fell short of her expectations. It seemed as if birthdays visited upon her some secret grief and made it impossible for her to be happy.

Part of me hoped for the best but most of me dreaded the worst. I feared that no matter what we did, this birthday celebration would leave her unhappy.

My husband drove with me to pick up Mom. She still lived in the same house we all grew up in. During the long drive to Columbus, my husband kept the conversation going. He asked about her life and got her talking.

She started telling stories I had never heard. Mom talked about how hard it was growing up on a farm with immigrant parents who couldn't read or write English. About how hard it was having three brothers go off to war for years, not knowing where they were. And how hard it was when her only sister moved out. Only she never used the word *hard*. It was just her life.

By the time we arrived at my sister's, I realized how little I knew about this woman who gave birth to me.

At the party, I placed the toy crown on her head and we called her Queen Mum. She wore that crown the whole day and smiled as if she really was queen for a day. We all chatted, ate cake, and then she opened gifts. My siblings knew just what she wanted, a dress, a blouse, a book.

Then I gave her the scroll about life in 1930 and she reminisced. She was born the year Nancy Drew started solving mysteries, Babe Ruth earned $80,000 a year, and Clarence Birdseye invented frozen food. That year, the planet Pluto was discovered and scientists predicted a man on the moon by 2050.

We all had a good laugh. Then, something came over me. Instead of handing her the gratitude list, I unrolled it and read it aloud.

"Seventy-five years!!! You have filled them with so many

gifts. For all of these, I thank you, and I thank God, for giving me you."

I thanked her for being a stay-at-home mom and forsaking any career she might have desired. For staying with Dad all those years when women all over the country divorced over the small stuff.

For filling our Easter baskets and playing the tooth fairy. For making every Christmas so magical we could hear reindeer on the roof. For giving us money to spend on each other at Christmas so we'd know the holiday was really about giving.

For teaching us how to change a diaper without poking the baby or ourselves. For breaking into spontaneous polkas in the living room. For introducing us to Perry Como, the Mills Brothers, and Mitch Miller. For humming happily in the kitchen, the best music of all.

For making homemade tomato soup, nut roll, and pigs in a blanket. For crocheting Christmas stars for our trees and afghans for our couches. For letting us watch the Three Stooges every day.

For waking us up for school every day, sometimes five times in one day. For that lovely penmanship on every school note that was too pretty to forge. For all the worrying she did for us when we forgot a school project, broke up with a guy, dated the wrong person.

For letting us use the empty dish detergent bottles for water fights. For not grounding us even when we lit firecrackers in the yard. For not always telling Dad on us.

For teaching us not to stand with the refrigerator door open because it wasn't supposed to be an air conditioner. For enduring our piano practices. For washing our hair in the kitchen sink before the bathroom had a shower. For exposing me to her favorite columnist, Erma Bombeck.

For healing our boo-boos with Bactine and a kiss. For unlocking the door at 2 a.m. and not asking any questions until morning. For all the worrying she did when we lost our homework or forgot our lunch.

For not letting us run with scissors or own a BB gun or stick out our tongues on cold metal in winter. For making sure none of us got hit by lightning, got blinded from having long bangs in our eyes, or wore dirty underwear to the emergency room.

For not kicking me out after learning I was pregnant. For being with me at the hospital when I went into labor. For babysitting my daughter while I spent years getting my life back on track.

For helping each of us to become our best selves. For forgiving us when we were at our worst. For praying for us when we didn't even know we needed prayers. For loving each of us equally, and never letting on that she loved me best.

Mom beamed as my siblings added to the list. It became a virtual lovefest as my brothers and sisters shared their own special moments and memories.

On the drive home my mom didn't say much. My husband played her life's sound track in CDs, Frank Sinatra, Nat King Cole, Ella Fitzgerald.

I didn't say much, either. I was thinking about that woman in the backseat. I never thought of her as the girl who once had to explain the telegrams to immigrant parents from Czechoslovakia when her brother Chuck ended up in a German prisoner of war camp, when her brother Mike contracted malaria on a mission across the sea. By the time she had turned ten, she was all alone on a big farm with parents who were strangers to America. How lonely she must have felt.

That Sunday night when we dropped her off, my mom seemed different to me. She looked like someone else, someone I could get to know. I told her I would see her tomorrow. The day after the party, Monday, was her actual birthday. I had promised to take her shopping.

But late Sunday night, my husband ended up in the hospital with kidney stones. I spent hours in the emergency room with him until he was admitted. I could easily have canceled the shopping trip. Mom would understand. She might not even care. But knowing she'd been let down so many times by life, I couldn't cancel. I was tempted, too. Partly because my husband was in the hospital, but mostly because I was afraid. I wanted to hang on to that fresh beginning with the woman I dropped off. What if I took her shopping and it all faded back to that painful blank slate?

I had to show up. I had made a promise. I drove an hour to get her, wondering the whole way how I would ever pull off a whole day of shopping. I hate malls.

When I picked her up at 10 a.m., she greeted me at the door all dressed up, a handbag matching her blouse, a string of pearls hanging from her neck. In the living room, she had turned the coffee table into a little altar. She had spread out a doily, set out flowers next to the birthday crown and the gratitude scroll. The daybook lay open on her desk. In it, for August 15, her birthday, she had written only one thing on the entire page: *shopping with Regina*. I swallowed my tears and my shame at having almost canceled.

So we shopped. She moved in slow motion, meandering through every aisle, looking at every blouse from collar to hemline. At first I grew impatient inside. Why was it taking so long to find an outfit? Then it hit me, my mom didn't care about what she bought. She wanted to spend time with me. So I slowed down. I took her to lunch, then drove her to two more malls. At the last store, she found a whole rack of clothes she loved. I bought her everything that fit.

Before taking her home, I insisted we get dessert. It was, after all, her birthday.

We sat outside in the sun eating scoops of Italian ice cream. To strangers, we looked like a mother and daughter who were the best of friends, chatting and laughing with ease. It was 5 p.m. We had spent a whole day together, just the two of us, for the first time in my life.

On the drive home, she confided that her parents never celebrated her birthday. The only memorable celebration growing up was when she turned 16, when her friends found out it was her birthday.

My mother thanked me for shopping, lunch, and dessert. She sounded more like a girl than a woman of 75 when she told me, "This is the best birthday I've ever had in my life."

No Matter How You Feel, Get Up, Dress Up, and Show Up for Life.

Almost every month, I have a day where I get stuck in the mud of me.

I used to blame hormones and PMS. After I hit 50, I blamed the lack of hormones. But men get stuck, too, so it must simply be the human condition.

One of my favorite singers, James Taylor, has a song called "Something in the Way She Moves." I can relate to the lyrics, about how every now and then the things we lean on lose their power to help us and we careen into places we shouldn't go.

We've all been to those places. We all have a personal pool of quicksand inside us where we begin to sink and need friends and family to find us and remind us of all the good that has been and will be.

I have my husband, daughter, and a couple of friends who

can usually reach me, but not always. On the truly rough days, it's hard to reach out to them to let them know I'm slipping away.

Those fragile days are handle-with-prayer days. I end up repeating the simplest prayer I can muster just to get out of bed. Some days it's a single Hail Mary. Other days, it's an entire rosary of them. I'll run through my spiritual artillery and use the Lord's Prayer or try the Serenity Prayer. I'll grab the Bible on my nightstand that seems to fall open to a passage of the Gospel of John that begins, "Let not your heart be troubled." One prayer by Thomas Merton often helps. He starts by admitting to God that he is lost and cannot see the way ahead and has no idea where he is going. I can relate.

When that doesn't help, I scramble and stumble through Psalms and affirmations and daily meditation books, exhausting the whole supply until I find relief. If I don't have enough strength, energy, or will to cling to God, right up front, I ask God to cling to me. I don't just ask, I tell God, "It's one of those days, God. The burden is on You, so hang on to me."

I once heard someone say that prayer is more than words. It's a stance you take, a position you claim. You throw your body against the door to keep the demons from advancing and stay put until they go away.

Over the years, I've developed a simple emergency response plan to use as soon as I feel the hurricane of those blue days blowing:

Have a 911 list of people who get it. Not the type A's who will tell you to suck it up and offer 20 ways to multitask your way through it, but people who know your favorite ice cream, candy bar, music, or movie to coax you back.

Avoid mean people, especially at work. And don't poke the gorilla boss. Stay away from the cage.

Don't do anything you don't absolutely have to do that day. Cancel anything that is negotiable.

Make no major decisions about your marriage, your career, your diet, or your self-worth. You are under the influence of a bad day. Don't analyze anything. Stay out of your head. It's not a safe place today.

Don't "awfulize" what you're feeling. The world isn't ending. You are just experiencing turbulence. The plane is safe. The pilot is good. You're in the right seat of life. You just hit a patch of bumpy air. Wait. It will pass.

I admit, on those rough days, I'm tempted to call off work and take a mental health day. Instead, I give myself permission to lower my standards for the next 24 hours. I take my friend Don's advice: Get up, dress up, and show up. Trim life down to its bare essentials.

Get up: Face the day vertical instead of surrendering to it horizontally.

Dress up: Put on your clothes, from head to toes. It triggers hope. I believe that's why, even in the poorest third-world countries, women adorn themselves with bright scarves, colorful beads, and glittering shells.

Show up: Most of life is showing up. It's a come-as-you-are day. To be a success, you do the best you can, which varies from day to day. My best today might suck, but if I show up, I've done the best I can do today.

If that's all you do, in the Olympics of life, you're a success. Getting up earns you a bronze medal. Dressing up gives you the silver. Showing up wins you the gold.

Once you do those three things, anything can happen. On some of my worst days I end up doing my best writing, parenting, loving.

Don, who taught me that motto, is one of the happiest people I've ever met and has had one of the hardest lives. He greets everyone with a loud "Yo!" and leaves each person with a hug and these words, "It's been a slice of heaven."

Don's had more blue days than most. When he was 11, his mother ended up in a mental institution. His dad was an alcoholic who couldn't raise the six kids. One Friday, Don was told he was going into an orphanage on Monday for three months. He didn't know he'd never, ever live with his family again. He was 16 the night a priest at the boys home broke the news that his mother had died from a brain aneurysm.

Years later, he lost a brother to alcoholism. His brother got into a fight. The other man won by hitting him with a car. Don's brother was in a coma for a month. Don always tells the good side of that story: God gave him 30 days to say good-bye to his brother.

Don became an alcoholism counselor. He married a nurse and they had two kids. Then his wife had an affair and the marriage unraveled. It broke something inside of him to see his family split up. Through it all, on those days when he didn't want to go to work, return calls, or listen to other people's problems, he practiced those words: Get up, dress up, and show up.

His words inspire me on blue days, which are now rare. No matter how I feel, I get up, dress up, and show up for life. When I do, the day always serves up more than I could have hoped for. Each day truly is a slice of heaven. Some days the slices are just smaller than others.

47

Breathe. It Calms the Mind.

If you want to get pregnant, try meditating.

I read that advice from a Harvard Medical School professor who reported that nearly 40 percent of couples in his research group who thought they were infertile got pregnant within six months after practicing meditation.

I think he left out something else they did.

Dr. Herbert Benson reported that uttering a few "ommms" a day helps keep the doctor away (but obviously not the stork). Chanting a mantra can also help relieve AIDS symptoms, lower high blood pressure, and prevent the need for some surgeries and medical procedures. Health insurers should cover meditation sessions to decrease the need for more costly treatments. Wouldn't it be great if health-care plans included a list of Buddhist monks among the network providers?

Meditation at its heart is being present with each breath

you take. I interviewed a professor once whose most important lesson plan was on breathing. When Christopher Faiver was a student at Hiram College in 1969, the university ran a round of talks called the Last Lecture Series. If you had one last lecture to give, what would you say? The idea stuck with him for decades. When he became a professor at John Carroll University, he gave a last lecture. He urged students to breathe.

Breathe?

He heard that some Eastern religions believe we have a finite number of breaths, and that we must use them wisely. He witnessed the power of breathing watching his grandson take his first breath and his mother take her last.

"I felt a sense of communion," he told me.

In his lecture, he spoke of all the people who helped him breathe easier, masters and mentors like Jesus, Buddha, and Gandhi, along with numerous teachers, colleagues, bosses, and students.

It made me think of the people who made me breathe easier, especially the man who introduced me to conscious breathing 20 years ago. About 50 men and women gathered for a meditation retreat that lasted from Friday evening to Sunday afternoon. I had gone hoping to meet a guy, as if the weekend were a spiritual singles' outing.

The presenter was a Buddhist monk who studied in Thailand. He was the kind of guy strangers look at and say, "He's a vegetarian." He was tall, gaunt, and wore baggy corduroy pants and Birkenstock sandals.

He told us to sit in a comfortable position, be silent, and listen to our own breathing. When he rang the bell, the meditation would be over. Listening to your breathing. How hard could that be?

I was excited at the chance to find a passport to peace. I expected to be transported to a quiet beach at sunrise or a mountaintop of utter calm or a lotus pond of tranquility. I expected something besides my crazy mind racing to and fro, bringing up images of everyone I ever hated or loved.

My mind was like a garbage dump. There was no peace. I daydreamed about my childhood, about my to-do list, about seeing people killed, about writing a book, about shopping for shoes. Then I'd catch myself and try to listen to my breaths. All I heard was a roomful of people sighing in frustration.

Finally, the bell rang. We got through the first session. The next day we meditated for 40 minutes at a stretch every two or three hours. It was agony. When the monk let us go outside for a walk, we were supposed to meditate, feeling our feet press into the earth in every step. We were to remain silent, even in the bathroom and at meals. Breathe, breathe, breathe. That was it.

Once outside, people were on the verge of mutiny. A group of five met under an oak tree and planned a rebellion. Four others packed up and went home.

The rest of the meditation sessions were grueling. It was like going back to the dentist to finish a root canal. My mind raced like a wild horse. To stay put and concentrate on breathing was torture. After 20 minutes of sitting, my mind screamed, "Ring the bell. Ring the $#%@ bell!"

After a whole day, I could count only to 15 before my mind took me to greener pastures. It drifted from the design in the curtains to a good-looking guy to memories of a summer vacation to unfinished work. My body ached from sitting still. I ended up exhausted from doing absolutely nothing.

By Sunday, half the people had already packed up their pillows, uncrossed their legs, and headed home. The monk closed the retreat by telling us that everything we ever needed to know was already within us.

"Then why did we come here?" someone muttered.

He could read our minds (after hearing the silent screams from us all weekend). "You are probably wondering what you will leave with," he said. Great wisdom? An overwhelming sense of God? Perfect harmony with the universe? Freedom from fear? A heart overflowing with love?

He told us about a student who asked the Zen master, "Why do you meditate? Does it make you a saint?"

"No," the master replied.

Does it make you more divine?

"No," he shook his head.

What, then, does it make you?

"Awake," he replied.

And how do you stay awake? You breathe.

LESSON
48

If You Don't Ask, You Don't Get.

T he hardest thing for me to do is to speak up.

I know, that's a little ironic considering I ended up writing a newspaper column for a living and speaking in front of 400,000 people. Guess the universe knows what I needed.

It also sent me a man who taught me how to find and use my voice. Before I met my husband, I was afraid to return a sweater, even with a receipt. I'd rather give it away to Goodwill than be hassled by a sales clerk about their returns policy.

My husband is the opposite. Bruce was born confident. When he wants something, he asks for it. He has no fear of rejection. He doesn't take it personally if someone says no. He can't figure out cowards like me. Why are we reluctant to ask?

Shame. We're ashamed to let others know we don't know something or that we need something. I grew up being taught

I had no needs. Whenever we wanted something, my dad always gave the same answer: You don't need it.

Pride. We don't want to give someone else the power over us to say no. We don't want to be made weak by rejection. We're afraid of how we will look to a perfect stranger who really happens to be an imperfect person just like us.

Fear. We're too afraid to speak up because it pokes a big fat finger in that old wound when the child in us heard no when it mattered most that someone say yes.

Guilt. We don't want to put anyone out. We're not deserving of their time, energy, and attention—even when that person is being paid to help us. We're polite to the point of paralysis.

My husband believes fear is something you feel before you jump out an airplane or scuba dive next to sharks. That I can understand, he says. He doesn't understand being afraid to ask a flight attendant for an upgrade. He can and does ask for anything and everything: An upgrade to first class. A better hotel room. A discount because he doesn't believe you should ever pay retail. Free refills. He'll even ask for directions!

Me?

Here's how pathetic I am. I can't ask the guy kicking my seat in an airplane to stop. I can't ask the people talking behind me in the theater to shut up. I get up and move. I'd go hungry before asking the stewardess for a vegetarian meal.

My worst moment? When my daughter was six, she had a handful of change to buy a bag of candy. I was standing in line at the grocery store conveyor belt and she set her pile of change on it. As we moved up in line, I saw a hand reach over and grab my daughter's change. It was a child of 12 or so. I caught her eye and stared at her. I didn't have it in me to stop her. She just stole my daughter's money, yet I couldn't even ask her for it or order her to put it back.

Years later, I took my nephew to a McDonald's. He got a root beer, drank it down, and asked for more. Do they have free refills? he asked. I'd find out. I took his cup to the counter. Before even opening my mouth, I turned into a chicken McNugget. I was too afraid of them saying no. I chickened out. Instead, I went over and filled his cup. Did I steal a refill? Might have. I don't know.

I'm starting to pay attention to people who ask. I'm noting mentally when it works. My friend Sharon took her five-year-old son to a basketball game. They had seats in the nosebleed section. As they climbed up and up and up, little Finnegan got scared. It was too high. He started to cry. Sharon spied some empty seats on the floor. She had three choices: force her scared child to sit in the ozone layer of seats, leave and go home, or ask for seats he wouldn't be afraid to sit in. She asked the ticket taker. He didn't know. He pointed her to someone else. That person pointed her to someone else. She kept asking. Finally, someone said yes. Finnegan got floor seats to watch the Cleveland Cavaliers and LeBron James dazzle the crowd.

One day I was out of my favorite Aveda shampoo. My husband and I stopped at the hair salon, but it wasn't open yet. It was 10:30. The store hours said it opened at 11 a.m. I said let's come back. My husband smiled. He saw it as a challenge. Just knock on the door and ask, he said. Nope. I couldn't. Sign says closed, I repeated. I'd rather go without it than ask and get turned down. He got that ornery grin, climbed out of the car, and went to the door. He knocked and yelled that he just wanted to buy shampoo. The girl inside shook her head no. He opened his wallet and held it up. She came to the door. We're not open yet so I can't take credit cards, she said. "I'll pay cash," he yelled through the glass. Next thing I know, he comes out with four bottles of shampoo.

After years of watching him speak up and reap the benefits, I finally spoke up in a big way. I wanted a raise. One day I prayed about it, had all my reasons mapped out in my brain, and went to lunch with the boss. I asked and he said no. But first, he humiliated me. I excused myself, went into the restroom, cried my eyes out, cleaned up, came back to the table, and changed the subject. Hours later at work, he said he'd find out what he could do. I got a small raise.

Years passed. I wanted a real raise. I had done my best work. Had he noticed? I wasn't going to assume he did. Never assume, my journalism professors taught me. One teacher dissected the word on the board: *ass u me.* "When you assume," he said, "you make an ass of u and me."

I sat down to think about why I deserved a raise. I typed up a good proposal and itemized the value I added to the paper, the newsroom, the company. I started the e-mail by telling the boss that I loved the job, the paper, the city. I thanked him for hiring me. I told him the importance of my position and that I was at the low end of the salary spectrum for my position. Then I pointed out the value I added to the paper in a long, itemized list with bullet points. At the end of the list, I asked for "a meaningful, significant raise."

I got one. Not only that, I got the exact amount I had in my head but had never named. Did I chicken out by asking in an e-mail versus in person? Maybe. But I asked, and I got.

You don't ask, you don't get. So ask. Sometimes the answer will be yes, sometimes it will be no. If you don't ask, the answer is always no. You already gave it to yourself.

49

Yield.

Wern e were losing Beth. Day by day, inch by inch, the life in Beth seemed to fade like a fragile ember that burns smaller and smaller until it goes out.

Diabetes had ruined both kidneys she was born with, then ruined the one stitched into her 14 years ago. Dialysis was her only hope, four hours a day, three days a week until she died or got a new kidney. She was on a waiting list and might have to wait four to six years to get one. My friend Beth would never last that long.

No one said it aloud, but we all thought it, we all knew it. We had said our prayers, but it's a hard prayer to say when you know that the gift of life your friend desperately needs will be the gift of life a stranger reluctantly surrenders.

No one said it, but we all feared that Christmas might be her last. For the past nine years, Beth and her husband, Michael, had shared Christmas Eve with us. The best Christmas Eve of all turned out to be that one when Beth wasn't at the table.

The phone rang after 11 p.m. the night before Christmas Eve. The call came in so late that we figured it was bad news.

It was the best news. There might be a donor for Beth.

Might.

Not just a kidney, but a pancreas, too. A pancreas meant Beth would no longer have diabetes. A new pancreas would produce insulin, something her 50-year-old body hasn't been able to do since she was ten. With a new pancreas, she wouldn't have to worry about losing her sight or her limbs to diabetes; she wouldn't have to worry about dying from it like her mother did; she wouldn't have to worry about not seeing her five-year-old daughter grow up.

Her husband couldn't believe it until she started packing her suitcase for the hospital. She had to pinch him—hard—so he knew he wasn't dreaming. Then he called one friend and the word went out and the prayers started up. "It's too good to be true, but please, Lord, let it be for me," Beth prayed.

We prayed for Beth, who works as a child life specialist at Rainbow Babies & Children's Hospital in Cleveland, where she had spent the last 18 years making children less afraid of needles and doctors and medical tests. We prayed for the family of the 21-year-old in Columbus who perished in a car accident, a family who, thank God, had the grace to yield in the face of grief and allow organs to be donated so someone else might live.

Beth and Michael dropped off their daughter, Michaela, at our house Christmas Eve morning at 6:30. Beth gave her a kiss in the dark and I hugged Beth and hoped for the best Christmas present of all: life.

Hours passed without a word. By 2 p.m., they still didn't know whether it was a match for Beth. Then the phone rang at 3 p.m. They were prepping Beth for surgery. A calm inside her dismissed the brief fear that she might not survive surgery. She focused on how wonderful life would be when she woke up and was no longer a diabetic.

All day we worried. Would her body be strong enough for the four-hour surgery? Would her body reject the organs? Would a little girl learn on Christmas Eve that her mom was healthier than ever or would she learn... we couldn't bear to finish that thought.

Little Michaela talked of Santa and the new Barbie she hoped he would bring and whether he would show up if she wasn't home and how reindeer could really fly. She believed wholeheartedly in the miracle of Christmas. Could we?

Then the phone rang. The pancreas was in. It was working. An hour later, we learned the kidney was good. Beth was peeing on the operating table. No more dialysis. No more insulin. The donor had been a perfect match. Beth had jumped to the top of the transplant list because out of all the people in the country on the waiting list, she was the closest match. The only thing closer would have been an identical twin.

Michael came back to our house and wrapped his arms around a little girl whose biggest Christmas wish was for a doll. He told her that Mommy wouldn't have to have any more "pokies" to check her blood sugar. As Michaela drifted off to sleep watching *Miracle on 34th Street*, her dad couldn't stop talking about the miracle on Cornell Road, the miracle in an operating room at University Hospitals, a miracle Michaela will hear about every Christmas.

I never knew there was another side of the story until I wrote a newspaper column about Beth's gift and got this e-mail from a woman who read the article.

I was touched by the front page story in the paper today. You see, my family also got a call from University Hospitals on Christmas Eve. My 31-year-old daughter is also on the transplant list there for a pancreas and kidney. She has had diabetes since the age of 8. She had cataracts at that time and had them removed. She has also had to have a toe removed and her kidneys started failing about four years ago.

She's been on the list for about 2½ years. We immediately called everyone we could think of to start a prayer chain for her. We also had all the emotions and hopes running through us as did Beth.

We knew that my daughter, Dawn, was second on the list. We knew that the first person on the list had to not match for her to get the gift of life. I must admit we prayed that the first person on the list did not match, but by 3 p.m. we also knew that she had. Dawn would have to wait again.

I would like to tell you that after 3 p.m. our prayers changed. We then started praying for the person that did match. I was so glad that the surgery was a success. I will continue to pray for Beth. Please let her know we are very happy for her. — Thank you, Sandra Whalen.

The e-mail blew me away. I picture that family huddled together praying for a miracle for their daughter and how hard it must have been when they found out they didn't get it. They didn't spend the next hours discouraged and disappointed, they made an abrupt U-turn and turned their prayers around for Beth.

How gracious to yield when so much is at stake. To pray for the person who would get the organs that would save your daughter's life. I barely find it in me to yield to a driver who wants to get in my lane on the highway or the person behind me on an airplane who needs to get off first to make a connecting flight. So many times I want what I want and can't see at all the small needs of anyone else around me, much less the big needs.

I had been so caught up in praying for Beth, I never thought to pray for the other person who was waiting for those organs. After that e-mail, I always wondered what happened to Dawn. Two years later, I ended up at an art show put on by patients at the Centers for Dialysis Care. One woman built a wall out of plastic medical tubing and red paper bricks to depict how it felt waiting for a transplant. The artist's name was Dawn Whalen.

Yes, *that* Dawn.

The art therapists had given each patient a camera to photograph a day in the life of dialysis. Dawn turned hers into a wall and wrote a song about undergoing dialysis three and a half hours a day, three days a week for three years. She glued photos on the wall of her blood test kit, the needles, the man who drives her to dialysis, the bottles of pills she takes.

Dawn was 32 but looked a perky 22, with short blonde-brown hair and long lashes. She couldn't stop smiling when I spoke to her. She got a kidney and pancreas transplant two years after Beth did. Her call came one Sunday morning. When she heard there might be an organ available and to stay close to be ready, she went to church and prayed for whomever would get the organs and she prayed for the person who had passed away. Then she got a phone call in church telling her to get to the hospital for the seven-hour operation.

Bless her heart, she comes back to the dialysis center to volunteer. Hundreds of people are still waiting, waiting for that perfect match—for someone to yield.

50

Life Isn't Tied with a Bow, but It's Still a Gift.

First my brother-in-law Randy sent an e-mail about it. Then a friend sent one. Then another. They all wanted to know if I knew the secret to life.

At first I ignored the e-mails and links, then figured perhaps the universe was trying to tell me something. What was the secret to money, relationships, and happiness?

It's not really a secret. You can trace it back to Plato, Beethoven, and Einstein. I can trace it back to my bookshelves, to Emmet Fox, Wayne Dyer, Ernest Holmes, and James Allen. To Matthew, Mark, Luke, and John.

There is one power. There is one law. No, not an eye for an eye, or always tip your server. The law of attraction. That's the secret. You attract everything that comes into your life by the thoughts you hold. You create your life with your thoughts.

You've heard, "You are what you eat." Nope. You are what

you think about all day. Scary, isn't it? Try thinking only good thoughts all day. I can make it an hour now without picturing doom and gloom, disease and pestilence. My brain is a fear factory. It churns out all kinds of nonsense. There's an ax murderer under the bed. A severed head in the clothes dryer. A live rat in the toilet bowl.

I read that Albert Einstein once said the most important question any human being can ask himself or herself is this: "Is this a friendly universe?" Of course not, I thought. Is he nuts? Actually, he was brilliant. Which made his question stick to me like Velcro.

What if I saw the universe as friendly? I started practicing. It was like seeing the world through new glasses. Think fear, you attract anxiety. Think abundance, you attract wealth. Think love, you attract compassion.

The secret isn't to master your boss, your bank account, or your kids. It's to master your mind. I pause now whenever I feel that cloud of doom over me and ask myself: What are you thinking? If you are feeling bad, change your thoughts, not your job, your clothes, your husband.

Einstein said, "There are only two ways to live your life. One is as though nothing is a miracle. The other is as though everything is."

Here's to miracles.

Now the thing about miracles is that you don't always recognize them. Sometimes they come in packages wrapped like big fat mistakes. The secret is to find the miracle in the mess. It's hard to do, especially if you are attempting to create a perfect you.

I've tried that. I listed resolutions in writing. Broke them into goals and objectives. Posted them where I could see them. Read them aloud. Breathed them in and out. Visualized them all happening.

I promised to eat more whole grains and less fat. Pay cash instead of using credit cards. Be a kinder spouse. Exercise every day. Then I systematically violated each resolution.

Most people resolve to get fit, lose weight, and eat right. They promise to quit smoking, drinking, and stressing out. They attempt to get out of debt, save more, and spend less. More advanced souls add this one: volunteer.

I heard a guy say that his whole life used to be centered on me, me, me. He was trying something new, making his life about we, we, we. The Jesuits call that being a man for others.

What can I do for others? Not earth-shattering plans that will overwhelm me into that abyss of almost doing good, but simple day-by-day, moment-by-moment actions. I once wrote about a guy named Don Szczepanski who lived that way. He was just a regular guy. Or so it seemed.

The path in life he took seemed ordinary enough. He drove the same route for 18 years, hopping in and out of a little white mail truck from 7 a.m. to 3:30 p.m.

Everyone in the tiny town of Avon, Ohio, called him Don the Mailman. He waved to people walking down the street and beeped the horn as he rumbled past. He gave tips on how to fix a troubled computer, shared the latest pictures of his grand-daughter, and was known to hand out samples of his home-made beef jerky.

He always carried stamps and always wore a smile. He delivered mail for 25 years, stopping by some 500 houses or businesses every day.

Then one day a neighbor named David noticed Don was missing from the route. When Don returned, he mentioned that something had shown up on a test. That was the last time Don would drive his mail truck.

Don had kidney cancer that had already spread to his lungs. The doctors said he would probably never leave the hospital. People started to call David, asking about Don. As word spread about Don's health, so did the stories. One parent told David how Don came to the door with the mail one day and noticed that one child had received some birthday cards, so Don added $5 to the stack.

Another parent told him how her son with cerebral palsy loved to greet the mail carrier. Don shut off the truck and let the boy climb in to see how everything worked. Don bought him a small postal truck for Christmas that year.

One neighbor kid shared how Don showed him the right way to throw a baseball and taught him to wear a baseball cap with the bill pointed "straight where you are headed, not to the side like a wise guy on TV."

The stories moved David to write to his neighbors:

Our friend (and the best mailman ever) is battling kidney cancer. Don has brightened many of our days with his warm smile and infectious laugh. It is time for us to return the favor. Please tie this blue ribbon on your mailbox so everyone can see it (especially Don!) and think of him for a moment in the middle of your busy day. Please consider dropping Don a note or a card. He will be touched by your thoughtfulness. Simply leave the cards in your mailbox (addressed to Don the Mailman) or bring them to the Avon Post Office.

Within days, 500 blue ribbons and bows dotted the town. Stacks of cards arrived for Don.

The day before Thanksgiving, Don was able to climb into his son's car and follow the route he had taken for 18 years. He got to see all those ribbons. He died a week later. He was 59. Friends celebrated his life with margaritas and beef jerky at a bowling alley.

Some people believe angels are supernatural beings with wings. Maybe they're ordinary folks like Don Szczepanski, delivering goodness along with the bills and postcards. Don didn't need wings. His wave carried him along just fine.

Don's life reminds me that it doesn't matter what we do for a living but how much life we put into our doing. My hairdresser Heidi constantly inspires me. One day she finished styling my hair, looked me in the eyes, and commanded like a preacher, "Go make something possible."

Make something possible.

A friend of mine signs her e-mails with a Leonard Cohen chorus discounting perfect offerings. She embraces her imperfect offerings of art and music, confident that any cracks in them let the light sneak in.

There's so much living to be squeezed into the cracks of one little day. You can make someone laugh, smile, hope, sing, think. The most important day of the year isn't Christmas or Easter, your anniversary or your birthday. It's the day you are in, so live the hell out of that day alone.

To do that means you will get messy, because life is messy. Yes, life is a gift, every day of it, but it isn't tied with a bow. Years ago, a Jesuit priest accused me of trying to live too carefully. He said it's as if I was given a beautiful party dress to wear but I'm so afraid to get it dirty, I sit out the party. No cake, no punch, no games for me. I don't want to get messy.

He was right. I was so afraid to fall, so afraid to fail, so afraid of life, I waited and watched from the sidelines. Not anymore. Cancer knocked that out of me.

I'm at the party, and I'm getting as messy as I can...and I just might be the last one to leave.

Author's Note

Dear Reader,

Thank you for buying and reading my first book. I hope this is the beginning of a long reading relationship.

If you were one of the thousands who passed along these 50 life lessons in e-mails to friends all over the world, thank you for inspiring me to go deeper and write this book.

I hope, too, you will continue to benefit from these lessons long after you have finished reading them. I'd love to hear how these life lessons help you along the way. Feel free to send me stories about how they changed your life. You can also pass along your own life lessons. My website, www.reginabrett.com, has a contact form for e-mails.

While you're there, enjoy my blog, columns, radio show podcast, discussion guide, tips for writers, favorite links, and photos, and learn about my next book.

A portion of my royalties from this book will support

The Gathering Place at www.touchedbycancer.org, which offers free services for anyone touched by cancer. To learn more about this amazing place, see www.touched.cancer.org.

I also hope you'll visit the Jesuit Retreat House, www.jrh-cleveland.org, the place I call my spiritual home.

Thank you again for taking the time to read *God Never Blinks*. I hope these lessons touch your life as deeply as they have mine and bring you greater joy.

All the best,

Regina Brett

www.reginabrett.com

Acknowledgments

I am eternally grateful for...

My parents, Tom and Mary, who sacrificed more than I will ever know to love and provide for their 11 children. They fortified us for life with their faith, hope, and courage.

The love and loud strength of my sisters, Theresa, Joan, Mary, Maureen, and Patricia. The love and quiet wisdom of my brothers, Michael, Tom, Mark, Jim, and Matthew.

My nieces and nephews, Rachel, Michael, Leah, Luke, Jaclyn, Laura, Emily, Hudson, Josiah, Anya, Erin, Harry, Jacob, Bill, and Brenda, who love me purely just for being Aunt Regina.

My sisters- and brothers-in-law, Tom, Chris, Tish, Andrew, Tom, Anita, Michelle, Randy, Gary, and Carol, who support me more than I deserve.

Mr. Ricco, my ninth-grade English teacher at Brown Junior

High. Sam Ricco taught me to love writing, one paragraph at a time.

The friends who gave me New Hope, especially Kathy and Bill Perfect, Melanie and Ed Rafferty, Judy and Michael Conway, Veronica Harris, and Don Davies. Their unconditional love made me whole.

My early mentors, Eileen Lynch, Barb Blackwell, Zoe Walsh, and Maura McEnaney, for trudging with me along the Road to Happy Destiny.

My endless circle of friends who cheer me on: Thrity Umrigar, Bob Paynter, Terry Pluto, Debbi Snook, Connie Schultz, Sue Klein, Karen Long, Tina Simmons, Jennifer Buck, Suellen Saunders, Marcie Goodman, Beth Segal, Michael Barron, Brendan Ring, and the staff at Nighttown. A special thanks to Sheryl Harris, my friend of friends, who listened to all my woes then ended most of them by finding me the man of my dreams.

The steadfast support of the Campbellville gang: Marty Friedman, Sandy Livingston, Michael Miller, Beth Ray, Peter Collins, Kris Anne Langille, Arlene and Buddy Kraus, Julie Steiner, and Dan Freidus.

Kent State University professors Bruce Larrick and Fred Endres, for leading me to journalism. Bill O'Connor and Susan Ager, for letting me stand on their shoulders to peer into the world of writing. Dale Allen, who made me a columnist at the *Beacon Journal*. Doug Clifton, who gave me a column at the *Plain Dealer*.

Stuart Warner, the best writing coach anywhere. He always valued my voice, even when it seemed to have laryngitis.

Plain Dealer publisher Terry Egger, editor Susan Goldberg, managing editor Debra Adam Simmons, and Barb Galbincea for giving me the freedom to do my best work and for granting permission to share it in this book. Dave Davis and Ted Diadiun for handling the endless requests to reprint these lessons. Jean Dubail, John Kroll, and Denise Polverine for shepherding my column and blog posts at www.cleveland.com. My colleagues at the *Plain Dealer* who daily harness the power of words to change the world.

Kit Jensen, Jerry Wareham, David Molpus, David Kanzeg, Bridget DeChagas, Paul Cox, Jeff Carlton, and the rest of the crew at Ideastream.

The endless constellation of newspaper readers whose e-mails, calls, and letters sustain me, who call Cleveland home: You are the hardest working, deepest believers in miracles any sports team could want. You really do rock.

Sister Mary Ann Flannery, for keeping the Jesuit Retreat House vibrant, and the wild women smoking outside all those Sister Ignatia Retreats.

Those honorable priests who dedicated their lives to saving souls: Father Joe Zubricky, Benno Kornely, Denis Brunelle, Jim Lewis, Joe Fortuno, Clem Metzger, and Kevin Conroy.

The angels in my Spirit Group: Ami Peacock, Gabrielle Brett, Sharon Sullivan, Beth Robenalt, and Vicki Prussak.

Ted Gup, who shared the greatest gift one writer can give another — the name and e-mail of his agent. His generosity led me to David Black Literary Agency, where I found my princess charming, agent Linda Loewenthal. David saw the spark; Linda fanned it into a fire. Her confidence still burns in me. She made every page of this book better and then found the perfect home for it.

Acknowledgments

The sentries at Grand Central Publishing who fiercely believed in this book. Publisher Jamie Raab whose passion for writing transformed this book. My editor, Karen Murgolo, who offered fabulous suggestions and possessed endless patience. Harvey-Jane Kowal and Christine Valentine for combing every inch of it. Diane Luger, who designed the best cover. Nancy Wiese, Nicole Bond, Peggy Boelke, and Matthew Ballast for making sure the rest of the world gets to read this book. Philippa "Pippa" White for her diligence to endless details.

Surgeon Leonard Brzozowski, oncologist Jim Sabiers, and nurse Pam Boone for saving my life.

My grandma Julia, whose love I felt first, last, and always.

My grandson, Asher, who will have my love following him everywhere.

The sons my husband brought to our marriage, Ben and Joe, for their patience and love as we created a new family. The son my daughter brought with her marriage, James, for making our family complete, and for taking the photo of me that graces this cover.

My compass, Bruce, who truly is my north, my south, my east, my west. No matter how many times I feel lost, he finds me. His love never fails, never falters.

My daughter, Gabrielle, who reminds me every day how much I am loved. She came along as a mystery and turned every day into an incredible blessing. She is proof that love alone matters most.

And the Source of it all, the God of my joy.

About the Author

Regina Brett is a columnist for the *Plain Dealer* in Cleveland, Ohio. She was born in 1956 and grew up in Ravenna, Ohio, population 12,000. She has a bachelor's degree in journalism and a master's in religious studies. She became a reporter in 1986. She has been writing columns since 1994.

Her articles have won numerous national, state, and local awards. She was named a Pulitzer Prize finalist for commentary in 2008 and in 2009. She also won the National Headliner Award for her columns on breast cancer in 1999 and in 2009.

This is her first book.

She lives in Cleveland, Ohio, with her husband, Bruce.

Her website is www.reginabrett.com.